THE INTELLIGENCE FACTOR

THE SMART SELLER'S APPROACH TO B2B PROSPECTING

ERIK FISHER

Lasting Press

ISBN: 978-1-949696-10-3 (mobi)

ISBN: 978-1-949696-11-0 (ePub)

ISBN: 978-1-949696-12-7 (paperback)

Printed in the United States of America

Published by:

Lasting Press

615 NW 2nd Ave. #915

Canby, OR 97013

Cover and Interior Design by: Rory Carruthers Marketing

Project Management, Book Development, Editing, and Launch by: Rory Carruthers Marketing

www.RoryCarruthers.com

For more information about Erik Fisher or to book him for your next event, speaking engagement, podcast or media interview, please contact erik@erikfisherofficial.com

CONTENTS

Preface   vii

Introduction   xiii

PART I
COLLECTING INTELLIGENCE

1. Your #1 Enemy: Fear   3
2. Better Business Conversations   17
3. The Sales Campaign   25
4. Ready, Aim, Fire: Defining Your Perfect Customer   33
5. Going Above the Power Band   43

PART II
VALUABLE INSIGHTS

6. The Most Important Factors of All: Problem Solving and Value Creation   61
7. Friend or Foe? Knowing Your Competition   71
8. Stop Being Anti-Social   81
9. Multiple Communication Medium Framework (MCMF)   89

PART III
BUILDING MOMENTUM

10. Don't. Get. Stuck.   95
11. Timing, Frequency, and Attempts   103
12. Messaging   115
13. Email Messaging Framework   123
14. Live Phone Messaging Framework   131

PART IV
PROSPERING THROUGH PROSPECTING

15. Calling with Confidence   165
16. Addressing Objections   173
17. Persistent Patience   185

Afterword   195
Acknowledgments   199
About the Author   201
Notes   203

PREFACE

In 1884, John Henry Patterson purchased the floundering National Cash Register company, the originator of the cash register, with a desire to turn it around. Many of his peers mocked him for making such a poor business purchase, and his friends and family thought he was crazy and would fail. In the five years prior to him purchasing the company, they had only sold about three hundred cash registers. But within three years of Patterson taking over the company, they had sold over three thousand cash registers. How was he able to turn around a company where the product was not in demand and had salespeople that actually prevented people from buying, even though they wanted a cash register? I'll get to that in just a moment.

Patterson is considered one of the greatest salespeople of all time and the father of sales. But by the 1950s, some of his strategies weren't as effective as they used to be. The invention of the television and post-World War II culture changed the landscape of sales. Sales became less about person-to-person conversations and more about making a connection through different forms of media, such as print, billboards, and commercials. David Ogilvy saw this shift happening and designed sales and ad campaigns that are still studied to this day. He became known as the master of the soft sell by utilizing long-form sales copy, brand-name recognition building, and eye-catching designs.

By the turn of the 21st century, there was another major shift in sales. Sales started to move from in-person sales and traditional media to online strategies. This opened up a whole new world of possibilities—the biggest being that you could reach almost anyone anywhere in the world with your sales message. Email became the most common form of sales communication. Pioneers of online sales and marketing, such as John Carlton, Frank Kern, and Perry Marshall, took the strategies that had worked over the past hundred years and utilized them to sell online. And it worked really well, for a time.

So, what do all of these sales pioneers have in common, and what made them so successful? A proper sales process. The problem is that what worked in the late 1800s and early 1900s didn't work as well in the 1950s. The strategies of the 1950s didn't work as well in the early 2000s. By the 2010s, many of the strategies that had worked so well offline and online started to work less and less everywhere. Prospects became more aware of sales tactics, which rendered them less effective. With every business jumping online to reach a global audience, competition saturated the market, leaving many salespeople struggling to get noticed in a sea of pitches.

Are you working with outdated sales models and wondering why you aren't hitting your targets?

Times are changing for salespeople as companies continue to leverage more marketing, sales automation, and efficiency tools. While I don't believe that artificial intelligence will completely take over the role of a salesperson, it will undoubtedly replace the average salesperson who merely follows up on leads who downloaded a case study or white paper.

The sales process has changed, and the digital world has taken over. Businesses no longer need salespeople early in the sales process. In today's online-focused business landscape, prospects don't need you until they're ready to make a buying decision. That is unless you bring them new and insightful information.

The companies and people we wish to conduct business with require a much different approach given the expanded reach they now have to acquire the information they need to make business decisions and whether or not to invest in products or services to help them realize their desired outcomes. A sales prospecting strategy that leverages data and information opens the prospect's eyes to new ways of thinking. New ideas, new thought processes, and different buying patterns create a more valuable experience in getting to the desired outcome.

Don't get me wrong, many of the strategies from the past are still effective and can be utilized in your sales process, but how you use them and when you use them has shifted so much that I developed a new sales system. This system is now responsible for over $40 million in sales and has transformed not only my life but the lives of those I've shared it with. That system is what I call the Intelligence Factor. A new way to sell where you're no longer looked at as a salesperson. Instead, you're looked upon as a trusted advisor or partner. That is one of the most influential and incredible positions you could ever be in as a salesperson.

What is the one thing that sets great salespeople apart from the average? If you said prospecting, you are right. In order to stay ahead of the continued digital advancement of AI, automation, and machine learning that works its way into sales and marketing organizations, it's imperative that you level up your sales prospecting methods and skills.

As a salesperson, effective prospecting should be the cornerstone of your sales and marketing strategy. It's what helps you build a consistent and full pipeline of future customers.

Discovery, positioning, anchoring, and many other key parts of an effective sales strategy are all very important. Still, if you can't build a large and consistent pipeline of business, they become nearly irrelevant. To be a successful salesperson in today's digital-driven market, you must be able to manage your time, display business acumen, and provide value in your messaging to prospects in order to gain their attention and earn their time.

More than 40% of salespeople find prospecting to be the most difficult part of their job, followed by closing (36%) and qualifying (22%).[1] There is a good reason you picked up this book. Prospecting is the most difficult part of the sales process. However, nothing solves poor sales results more than a big fat pipeline due to phenomenal prospecting!

Salespeople who leverage the Intelligence Factor will thrive in the next decade to come, while those stuck in old habits and strategies will flounder, hoping and praying that they can hit their sales numbers and make a living wage. Sadly, those who don't leverage a modern-day approach will continue a pattern of jumping from company to company, eventually leaving their career in sales behind to find something less challenging that requires less work.

When you utilize the strategies outlined in this book, every part of the sales process becomes easier. You become a trusted advisor to your clients. They come to you looking for solutions. You earn more money, and your clients are happy. That's the Intelligence Factor.

The Intelligence Factor shows you how to master phenomenal prospecting by intelligently using research and data to:

- Build Your Confidence in Prospecting
- Identify Your Ideal Prospect

- Communicate Effectively with Prospects
- Bring Value and Insight to Your Prospects
- Find Phenomenal Success as a Salesperson

As a bonus, I am sharing the Intelligent Sales Secrets Academy's *Ready. Aim. Fire Workbook.* This workbook includes powerful exercises that will help you apply the concepts in this book to your own prospecting. Go to www.TheIntelligenceFactor.com/freeworkbook now to get this fantastic bonus!

INTRODUCTION

When I first started in sales, I struggled badly. I feared rejection like the plague and couldn't handle an objection if my life depended on it. Although I was struggling, I initially refused to listen to any advice from the successful salespeople I knew. Instead, I continued to make excuses about why I wasn't hitting my sales numbers.

I can still vividly remember all my mistakes and excuses. I also remember how those excuses prevented me from making a living in sales. I remember being unable to afford my small studio apartment in downtown Chicago. As I watched my boss and a few of my peers earn six-figure incomes in their early twenties, my envy grew.

In my heart, I knew that sales was where I belonged. I wanted to provide the ideal life for myself and my future family—a life with few financial limitations, plenty of opportunities, and the ability to be philanthropic both financially and with my time. I knew I had to change the way I was doing things. I had to become really honest with myself about why I was not hitting my goals. I was self-sabotaging almost every aspect of my life, but it was my unwillingness to listen to those who were getting the results I wanted that held my sales career back the most. It wasn't until I found and applied the strategies of top sales earners that I turned the corner.

Hard Work and Heartbreak

I grew up in a typical household in northern Illinois. My mom and dad were both educators. My dad was a high school principal, and my mom was a German teacher. They were loving parents, but I had low self-confidence because I didn't believe I was really good at anything. In school, I found a love of sports with soccer and basketball, which started to bring me out of my shell. I wasn't a naturally talented athlete, but I was extremely competitive. During high school, I realized the one thing I could control was the effort and time I put into practicing my craft and conditioning. I took pride in my work ethic and physical conditioning. It was a big confidence booster for me as I saw my labor come to fruition in practices and games. At the time, I didn't realize that all my confidence was tied to being an athlete.

When I graduated high school, I dreamed of staying in shape and playing college soccer. Unfortunately, that dream came to an end after I ended up having knee surgery from a basketball injury. Like many kids, I dedicated many years of my childhood to something that I took pride in and dreamed of playing college sports to feed my competitive spirit. When you work really, really hard for something, when your whole sense of self-worth and confidence is tied to that thing, and you lose it all, it's devastating. I completely lost the confidence I had built up through sports and felt like I didn't really fit into this brand new environment.

This loss of confidence and feeling of disconnect led to a lot of bad decision making. I partied my way through my freshman year of college and was pulled out of school by my parents because my grades were so poor. This was only the beginning of my downhill journey.

After dropping out of college, I got a job at a telemarketing company selling customers long-distance phone lines. I quickly realized the caliber of people I was working with was exactly what you would expect a telemarketer to be. They were all non-college graduates who lived less than desirable lives; nonetheless, they were incredibly hard workers, and many were very good at sales. I made $30,000 working part-time in the first year at the job with no degree. I thought I was on top of the world.

Unfortunately, I continued to make bad decisions. I spent every dollar partying. My parents and I were not getting along. I was spending time with the wrong crowd. I even got in trouble with the law a few times. I firmly believe I was one bad decision away from either being behind bars or not being here on Earth. I needed to find a new path.

I knew if I was going to make things right with my parents, I had to get my college degree. I went to a community college for a year and had to get near-perfect grades if I wanted to get into the Illinois State University College of Business. I was determined and motivated, and I was able to achieve my goal of getting accepted into Illinois State.

A New Start

While I was in college, a career in sales was still in the back of my mind. I saw the possibility sales could provide, so I got a job selling suits for a department store. To them, it was sales. At the time, I thought so too. Looking back now, I realize retail sales isn't really a sales job since people are coming in to buy something. However, I was able to earn commission and learn how to upsell the customer or increase the number of suits they purchased that day. I liked helping people feel good about their purchases. I did pretty well and was recognized as one of their top sales reps at the store.

When I graduated college, I got a job at one of the oldest US banks. I landed the job because my boss and I went to the same high school and college. I owe him a tremendous amount of gratitude for inspiring me to be a great salesperson. I saw the effort and discipline he put in and how he was able to talk to prospective customers about different mortgage options for their homes. He was an exceptional salesperson, and he really was the primary reason I moved forward with sales as a career. He was making a significant six-figure income in his mid-twenties, and I wanted a lot of what he had.

I realized if I wanted what he had, I had to do everything he did. I got to the office early to get a jump start on my day. I packed my own lunch and ate it at my desk to save money and allow for more time to work. When he was making calls, I made sure I was on the phone making calls as well. He never walked anywhere in the office unless there was a business purpose, so I stayed at my desk and resisted the urge to waste time. He stayed later than everyone in the office even though he was the highest earner, so I figured that was a good idea as well.

With my newfound habits, I practiced my craft an incredible amount and got better and better. It made a world of difference in my results. I ended up going from thinking I was going to quit that job because it was so hard to managing an office and making the six-figure income I dreamed of at the age of twenty-five.

My World Turned Upside Down

Then the financial meltdown happened, and the bank was asking us to do things that I really didn't feel comfortable with. I knew I had to change directions. The economy was falling apart with no end in sight, and sales positions in the mortgage industry weren't available. At this point, I had a choice to make. Either find a new profession or find a way to be successful in sales, no matter the industry. It wasn't an easy decision with the economy in such turmoil and the job market so scarce, but thankfully, I decided to go all-in on sales.

Shortly after I decided to go all-in on a career in sales, a long-time friend of mine recommended I apply to the company he was working for. As I came into my interview, I pulled out every single award I had been given at every single sales job I had ever had. The office director who hired me still laughs to this day because I brought in a huge binder with a plethora of awards and data that showed I was the number one rep in the company or region at various times throughout the last year. It came off as extremely arrogant, but it was social proof that I was amazing at sales. I had hoped it would convince them to hire me, and it worked.

When I joined my new company, I was the young whippersnapper who thought he knew everything. I thought that the people I worked with knew nothing about sales. In my eyes, I was the award-winning sales guy who was going to come in and show them how it was done. Thankfully, I had a lot of coworkers who set me straight while also welcoming me. It has always been a company of honest feedback. My new coworkers told me, "It's ok, you don't need to know everything." While I had some things to work on, they noticed I was very motivated, had a tremendous amount of desire, and a strong work ethic.

I did the math and thought if I could just work harder than everybody else and get more reps in, that would get me to a level where I was at least earning close to the money I had been making at the bank. This didn't end up being the case.

Over the course of the first year, we were still in a

recession. I literally made no commission that year, and it was rough, to say the least. Somewhere along the line in 2009, the economy started recovering and business changed. I realized that good old fashioned hard work gets you pretty far in sales because it's the stuff most people don't want to do. I learned a lot that year through experience and from another amazing mentor. He taught me a valuable lesson that I'll share in this book and has been a major reason I've been blessed with the success I've had over the years.

If you just outwork other people, you can usually get into the top 10% of whatever your industry is, but it won't get you into the top 1%. You have to be intentional in your sales process and tactics if you want to be in that club. The people I wanted to be like were the millionaires at the company I worked for. What was it that they were doing? How were they using their time? Where were they focusing their energies? You'll discover all that and more as you go through this book.

As I mentioned before, the strategies I developed and am sharing in this book have been responsible for over $40 million in sales and have transformed not only my life but also the lives of those I've shared it with. I am very proud of the success I have achieved in my career, but more than anything, I'm eternally grateful. I'm thankful that I found a way for a very average guy to find wonderful people and an organization that provided the vehicle to achieve many of my life goals. With that said, with all my life's failures, I have never lost one thing: belief in myself. Belief that I would someday be great at something and do great things for others.

Implementing The Intelligence Factor

To receive value and the desired results from this book, you must implement what you learn consistently over an extended period by putting the suggested practices to work.

This is not a "get rich quick" book, as those tactics yield short-term results and harm your overall brand and relationship with your market and customers.

This book is not a list of 300 pre-baked scripts you can use to open doors, handle objections, or close a customer.

Generally speaking, pre-baked scripts don't work in professional B2B sales any longer.

If your goal is to show up with your customer as a cheesy salesperson from 1980, then by all means, continue asking your customers, "What Keeps You Up at Night?"

Of all the sales content I've consumed, I've still yet to find the "secret sauce" that every sales guru is selling. That's because there is no "secret sauce." Most sales content is riddled with promises of perfect scripts that will help you open more doors and close more deals.

I wrote this book so that salespeople like yourself could begin implementing these methods on day one and start seeing results quickly. The book is laid out in the exact process and methodology I follow when I'm entering a new territory, enterprise customer, or niche. It requires effort, but it works. The results you get can be life-changing, like they were for me.

As you read through the book, you'll see several exercises laid out for you in most of the chapters that correspond to a free downloadable workbook. The *Ready. Aim. Fire. Workbook* is filled with exercises that are intended to be used in real-life scenarios in your business. You can download it at www.TheIntelligenceFactor.com/freeworkbook.

If you follow the strategies in this book and complete the exercises in the workbook, you'll be well on your way to seeing the success you deserve by building strong relationships, becoming a person of authority, and growing your sales pipeline.

Are you ready?

Let's begin!

PART I

COLLECTING
INTELLIGENCE

1

YOUR #1 ENEMY: FEAR

In 2005, I was selling mortgages for a large, reputable US bank. The culture was strong and filled with eager young salespeople fresh out of college hoping to hit it big. I had joined the company after experiencing success in low-level sales jobs in the past. While none of my prior work would be considered *professional selling*, I knew what I was getting into, and I knew it would be hard at first.

When I graduated from college, I had zero debt thanks to my amazing parents, yet I still found a way to dig myself into a financial hole due to poor decision making. I worked long hours, working from 8 AM-7 PM most days. I did what most recent college grads did. I worked, partied, worked some more, and partied even more. The problem was, I had no substantial income other than the small salary I was earning, which barely covered the rent of my studio apartment in Chicago's Gold Coast neighborhood. Each week, I was further deflated and scared that I was going to end up bankrupt or worse due to the negative cash flow situation I had put myself in. Regardless of my financial situation and an absolute need to make more money, I was terrified of picking up the phone and calling prospective customers. How can you earn money in sales if you don't prospect?

When I look at the times when I had my toughest years, it was because I was scared. I was scared of failing. I was scared of people telling me no, and when they did, I took it personally. If you fear rejection on a daily basis, I want to tell you that that's okay—temporarily. What's not okay is staying paralyzed in that moment and never taking action.

Through all the ups and downs in my career, the times that I succeeded were when I stopped the fear of rejection right in its tracks. In fact, it wasn't until I understood how to leverage fear that I started seeing exponential growth.

Fear of Rejection

By far, the number one obstacle preventing salespeople from finding success is their ability to overcome their fear of rejection. Before we talk about how we can get over our fear of rejection, we need to understand what fear is. If you think about the concept of standing on the edge of a bridge, 10,000 feet above a treacherous river, the fear you feel of falling is very real. However, there is a difference between fear and danger.

In fact, in this circumstance, sensing danger is what prevents us from falling to our death. However, what you need to understand when it comes to sales is that the fear of taking risks is what holds us back. If you can't understand why it's holding you back, it's very difficult to overcome it.

A lot of this advice has been given by other sales leaders and businessmen throughout the years. However, I've put together a concise list of what I'm able to do in order to overcome my fear, tie myself back to my *why*, and stay motivated.

What Is Fear?

First, let's talk about what fear really is so that we can better understand it. Fear has two components—the biological and the physiological. The physiological reaction is a chemical reaction that takes place when your body senses a stressful stimulus, which sends a series of signals to the thalamus in your brain. It's basically like a telephone switch, and it's dialed directly to the amygdala, which releases neurotransmitters throughout the body, notably glutamine, the chemical behind fear. This is what causes a rapid heartbeat, fast breathing, and tense muscles, amongst many other reactions. You may also know this as the fight or flight response.

The other component of fear, or better yet the fear of rejection, is very biological. I really like the way that sales trainer, author, and owner of SalesGravy Inc., Jeb Blount, describes the biological component to fear:

> [O]ur primal fear of rejection dates back to mankind's early days hunter-gatherers, in which survival was dependent upon being accepted by the tribe.
>
> The vulnerability we feel from the prospect of rejection is what keeps many people from simply asking for what they want, be it something as trivial as a drink refill or as important as a pay raise.
>
> 'The only way to avoid being rejected is to never ask for anything again,' he said. 'Which is why there are so many people... who did not achieve what they could have achieved because they simply didn't ask.'
>
> ...rejection is the only emotion the body treats as a physical injury. So strong is the fear of rejection that [Blount has] met combat-experienced military recruiters who said they were more comfortable taking fire than cold-calling 17-year-olds.[1]

How to Overcome Fear

Now that you understand the psychology behind fear and recognize that it's just a chemical reaction, you need to realize what you can do to stop it.

Fear is tied to the unknown. The what-ifs. The number one thing I would like you to remember is this—fear cannot kill you.

Several years ago, I happened to bump into one of my company's executives at an airport restaurant. As we shared in small talk, we discussed the training I had just gone through, and he told me about a sales leader he was coaching through a very large negotiation with a Fortune 100 client.

The sales leader he was coaching was fairly new to his leadership job, but extremely talented, bright, and confident. I was very surprised to hear that he was scared, because typically he had no fear. He is also one of the smartest sales leaders I've had the opportunity to work with. Nonetheless, as the story went on, he continued to tell me that as they were preparing for the meeting, he continued to sense the *what-ifs, I'm not sures,* and *what's going to happen?* He said he could feel the fear in the sales leader's voice.

What he ended up realizing was he was just fearful of what would happen if they said no. If they didn't sign on the dotted line. This is what he had told the sales leader: "What are you so worried about? They ain't gonna eat ya!" I'll never forget that.

The reason I share this story is that everybody feels fear at some point in their career. Nobody is alone. Any sales guru who tells you they've never had any fear in their life is lying to you. Remember, fear is a chemical reaction in your brain. What it boils down to are several signals and pathways in our brains that force us to stop dead in our tracks when there's an action we're about to take that has an unknown outcome.

With all of the concepts that I write in this book, your

ability to get over your fear of rejection and the anxiety you feel from it will be the number one contributor to you either succeeding or failing in your sales career.

Fear is often connected to anxiety. So you need to figure out how to get over that anxious feeling when your heart rate starts beating or you're worried about what the outcome is going to be of a particular sales call or meeting.

There have been times in my career when I've felt fear, yet I've been able to overcome it, put an end to it, and start moving forward and focus on the right activities.

Here are five strategies that have helped me push through fear and into productivity. If fear is holding you back, use the information below to flip fear on its belly and continue to take action.

1. Go for No. Game-ify prospecting. Flip it on its head and start trying to get more "nos." Why? Because if "no" becomes the goal, you change the response in your brain. "No" becomes a very positive trigger. Try to get as many nos as you possibly can and turn rejection into something positive.

Set a goal for yourself to get fifty "nos" a day. Over time, and by practicing this for weeks on end, you will no longer consider "no" to be a negative trigger. It will become a positive trigger—something you are no longer afraid of and can overcome. In fact, it often makes sales prospecting oddly fun because you're changing the game for yourself.

2. Run Straight at Fear. I've heard this from several sales leaders over the course of all the years that I've been consuming sales knowledge, and this piece of advice is by far the one that I feel ties most closely to the psychology and the chemical reaction to fear. When fear is triggered in our mind chemically, the longer that we persist and

marinate in that fear, the bigger it grows. Think about that for a second. I'll use the standing on the bridge example again. If you're standing on the edge of a bridge, 10,000 feet above a fast moving and rock-filled river, the longer you stand on that edge, the more that fear consumes you. In fact, your anxiety increases, your blood pressure increases, and eventually you won't jump.

Now, I'm not saying you should be jumping off a bridge, but what I am saying is, how often are you paralyzed by fear? How often are you too afraid to pick up the phone or send an email or text message to a customer because you're afraid of their response? If you don't take action right away, what happens? I think you know the answer. Nothing. So the advice I would give you for number two is this: run straight at fear. The minute you feel the chemical reaction of fear and anxiety, do exactly what it's telling you not to do. If you're about to embark on calling an executive at an organization you're targeting, assuming you've done the research outlined in this book, call that executive. Don't worry; nothing is going to happen to you. They're not going to eat you! Chances are they likely won't pick up the phone anyway, but if they do, you have your chance to set up a great appointment. If you never try, you will never know in the first place.

3. Don't Avoid Income Producing Activities. Fear of rejection often leads to us avoiding stressful situations completely by focusing on other tasks. If you're struggling to overcome rejection, I want you to think about this. What percentage of your day are you spending on income-producing activities?

An income-producing activity would include calling a customer, emailing a customer, sending a text message, meeting with a customer, preparing a proposal, or reaching out via social media. What percentage of your day are you doing those activities?

Anytime I saw lower sales numbers, it was because I was spending too much time on non-income producing activities. So let's talk about those: doing too much research, chit-chatting with coworkers in the office, walking around, embarking and partaking in activities like getting coffee, scrolling social media, walking to the bathroom, and stopping and talking to the secretary. If you're driving to a meeting, stopping on your way back from that meeting to get gas and get a coffee, or listening to music on the radio, those are all non-income producing activities. I know it may seem a bit of a polarizing perspective, but it's true.

In this book, you'll find that I focus heavily on research and the importance of being extremely prepared, essentially following a blueprint and a strategy that allows all sales outreach to become much easier for you. However, I would encourage you to do much of your research and preparation during non-business hours. You might be saying to yourself, "Well, I don't want my entire life to be focused on business. I've got a life to live. I've got children, I've got a spouse, I want to hang out with my friends." Listen, you're no different than anybody else. The way that I've been able to scale my business over the years is by being willing to do the things that nobody else has been willing to do.

When everybody wants to leave the office and go to happy hour, I stay and do customer research, or perhaps I make customer calls. Early on in my career, I would go home, work out, make dinner, and then I would enjoy a cocktail of my choice and do customer research in the evenings, building my prospecting list for the coming weeks. This allowed me to focus on what was most important when I was in the office—customer outreach.

Salespeople I've worked with who failed are the ones who get overly consumed with research during their day. They want to feel productive while avoiding their fear of rejection. They find every excuse to not make sales calls. They get stuck, so they spend hours upon hours doing diligent research, trying to read articles about sales, and trying to read articles about the customer they're eventually going to call. They take forever to type lengthy emails. Your customers don't want to read a book of an email. They don't have time. So why are you spending all your time writing long emails when they are just going to end up deleted or in their junk folder?

Ask yourself where you're spending your time during the day. If you're spending the majority of your time typing emails and researching customers from 7:00 AM to 6:00 PM, stop for a minute and think about what's holding you back. Why are you afraid to pick up the phone and make twenty to thirty sales calls over the course of an hour? Why is the majority of your time not spent focusing on calling your customers and reaching out to them?

4. Manage your time before your time manages you. Although many salespeople avoid prospecting due to their fear of rejection and discomfort, the majority of your day and your time in a sales role should be focused on pursuing customers. Take control of your fear by prioritizing prospecting on a daily basis.

Every successful person I've ever worked with runs most of their life according to a calendar. Your calendar is your best friend. Prevent yourself from procrastinating and avoiding prospecting by creating scheduled time blocks for prospecting calls or other forms of outreach. Without a schedule, you have no plan. Without a plan, you are destined to fail because your fears will take over and prevent you from using your time effectively.

Most salespeople simply limp through their workday, trying to be productive while avoiding the tasks that make them uncomfortable. They aren't intentional with how they are spending their time and end up procrastinating. They get into the office, grab some coffee, and sit down at their desk. An email comes through, so they respond to it. Somebody calls them, so they take the call. A friend sends them a text, so they reply. Soon, it is time for lunch. They take an hour lunch with coworkers. On the way back to their desk, they stop and talk to a few more coworkers. I think you're getting the point. The amount of time wasted by salespeople is unbelievable.

You need to set a schedule and a daily plan for yourself every single day. I believe that the best way to do this is to set your day up where you're making sales calls early in the morning. Get up at 5:00 AM and from 5:30-6 AM, send prospecting and follow-up emails so they're fresh in your prospects' inboxes when they check their email. Then continue with your morning routine. Get yourself to your office, or home workspace if you're working remotely, and then from 7:30 AM to 8:30 AM, before your customers are busy, start doing customer outreach via phone and text message.

If you put it on your calendar and stick to your schedule, you are managing your time, your effort, your fears, and your goals because you are the one in control. Time and fear are no longer controlling you. If you let them have control, you will end up repeating the same avoidant behavior over and over again.

5. Set extremely lofty goals for yourself and tie them to your *why*. Many of you are in sales because you want to drastically change your life financially. I know that was my reason, but it goes deeper than that. For me, I wanted to prove to my parents that I was going to make something of myself. As I grew older, got married, and had children of my own, my entire life purpose changed. Therefore, my *why* is now tied to taking care of my own family.

If your *why* is that you want to make more money, why is that? Do some digging to understand what's most important to you. Maybe it's because you want to be able to take care of your parents, travel the world, or donate money to your favorite charity. Find your *why*, write it down on a piece of paper, and paste it on your desk, your cubicle, or on the mirrors in your bathroom as a daily reminder of your *why*, the reason you're showing up, and how you're showing up every single day.

In addition to knowing your *why*, I believe it's imperative to have massive goals. Goals so big that your family, friends, and co-workers think you're a bit crazy. Massive goals will guide you and give you direction. Most of us have been advised to set S.M.A.R.T. goals. Goals that are specific, measurable, achievable, realistic, and timely. There is nothing wrong with using this method of goal setting. In fact, I would encourage you to use the S.M.A.R.T. method as it nearly always yields positive results.

However, massive goals are audacious, scary goals. If you are really setting goals of this magnitude, it should create some self-doubt because they seem unachievable. There are many reasons why big goals are important, but to me, it's because it becomes our anchor. It's the thing we dream about, envision, and write down that nobody thinks we can achieve. It's also the goal that helps us through shorter sprints of challenging times. Massive goals dwarf fear. We realize that overcoming fear is part of the equation and learn to expect it as part of the large goal-setting process.

If you remember what your *why* is and set massive goals tied to your purpose, they will help you overcome your fear.

The Power of Why

To illustrate the power of *why*, I'd like to share a story of a young woman I've worked with for the past five years. This young woman had worked in retail for a number of years, and we had hired her through a referral, but she didn't really have any true enterprise sales experience. As I stated from my own experience, in retail, there's really not a whole lot of selling that happens, other than helping a customer make a decision on something they've already come into the store to buy.

When we hired this young woman, she started in an internal sales role which required her to sell to the outside salespeople. With little experience, she was extremely assertive. To be frank, I remember she really got on my nerves at first because her messaging was off. She didn't really know what she was talking about, but she kept on being persistent. It was almost as if she didn't care what the outcome of our conversations were; she just kept plugging along. However, through all the repetitions of trying and failing, trying and failing, she started succeeding. It became the law of averages. She would try and fail ten times, and then she would win. Over time, she kept winning more and more.

Eventually, we ended up promoting this young woman into an outside sales role. She was incredibly inexperienced when it came to sales calls. She didn't know exactly what to do or what to say as she called customers and ran into objections, but she kept taking consistent action. Little did she know, her inexperience was her secret weapon. It was almost as if there was no fear in her mind. It was like the chemical reaction didn't happen. She took action consistently on a daily basis and never hesitated.

This young woman, who I'm proud to call a colleague and friend, has grown the fastest in terms of total sales production of anyone I've ever worked with in the twelve years of working for my company. She's now one of the top sales producers in our organization, one of the top sales producers in our region, and making a significant income, which has completely changed her life.

She was able to stop fear in its tracks because of her *why*. I strongly believe that the reason for her success is because she has an extreme sense of purpose. She definitely understands why she's in the role she's in. She's had some challenges in her life, many more than I've ever experienced, and that's part of the reason why I admire her so much.

The troubles and challenges she's endured have built up a bulletproof vest. She's been able to handle pretty much anything that's thrown at her. By far, the number one reason why she's been able to grow and expand her business as much as she has is that she focuses on income-producing activities over and over and over again and doesn't get stuck in paralysis by analysis. And of course, the consistent repetitions turned her into a highly skilled salesperson.

Facing Your Fears

To close out this chapter, I'd like you to remember a few key points. Fear is a chemical reaction in your brain. Nothing more, nothing less. Nothing is happening to you physically other than the chemical trigger that's occurring in your brain. Change the game and flip fear on its head. Start focusing on getting more nos instead of focusing on getting more yesses. Instead of yes being a positive trigger in your mind, you'll now be searching for more "nos." Face your fears right away. Build your schedule and manage your time, don't let your time manage you. Know your *why* and use it to defeat your fears.

As you work through your days, weeks, and months, don't let fear be the reason you don't take action.

2

BETTER BUSINESS CONVERSATIONS

While I feel that fear of rejection prevents salespeople from prospecting and limits their ability to drive sales, sales messaging is just as important. If you're struggling with your prospecting and sales efforts, poor sales messaging is likely the major reason you aren't seeing the success you desire.

A Way to Better Business Conversations

Sales prospecting—working the deal through your pipeline and closing a deal—requires strong relationship building skills. Many salespeople struggle to build meaningful relationships because they lack the ability to build trust with their prospects. You must earn trust through insight, education, and showing up with your customer in a way that is meaningful to them. In order to build that trust, you must understand your customer. Plain and simple.

These days, businesses are extremely dynamic. Every business I've worked with operates differently, but there are many things they do that are the same. Having an overall understanding of how businesses evaluate business needs, research solutions and products that they want to purchase to solve business problems, engage with suppliers or partners, and ultimately, finalize contractual agreements is extremely important.

In today's sophisticated and digitally-driven B2B market, businesses and decision-makers no longer want or need to engage with salespeople; they'd rather do their research online. While this is different for every type of business, and certainly smaller businesses may make most of their purchases via online mediums, large enterprise businesses still do plenty of their research through online forums, advisors, subscription services, and leveraging their networks.

Speak Their Language

In order for you, as a salesperson, to become valuable to the decision-maker early on in the sales cycle, you must show up differently. Prospects and customers expect more from sellers in today's market. If you can't speak their language, you don't deserve to talk to them. If you don't understand how small, medium, and enterprise large businesses make decisions, you are an impediment to their business. You're not an asset. Essentially, if you call a customer or a prospect, and you are not immediately providing valuable insights or a thought-provoking question to them, you are just wasting their time.

Customers want to engage in dialogue with those who not only understand their business, but also speak their language. What does that mean? Well, if you're speaking to an IT department, and you're specifically speaking to someone in information security, you better understand what's important to an information security leader. Conversely, if you're selling SAAS software to HR leaders, you better understand all the challenges that exist for an HR leader, as well as how they can leverage an SAAS-based solution to accomplish their objectives.

Business acumen helps sellers engage in meaningful conversations as they perform outreach with prospects and current customers. Sellers with business acumen understand how companies make decisions as part of their business cycle. When you understand a business cycle in a B2B sales pursuit, it allows you to become more calm and collected, and it removes unnecessary and unproductive pushy behavior that turns off most modern-day decision-makers. You see, they can sense that you are trying to close the deal.

Of course, there is nothing wrong with asking the business to close the deal! However, in my experience with B2B sales, high-pressure closing tactics bleed desperation, and in many cases, the prospect will take notice and ultimately not want to do business with you. There's a better way.

Be an Educated Seller

A more educated and informed seller is a more powerful seller, and they can quickly grab a customer's or prospect's attention. Think about this for a minute. If you sell HR software, and you're calling into an organization, which of the following do you think would better grab the prospect's attention?

Example one: "Hi Mr. Customer. I'm reaching out to you today because we help large organizations streamline their HR processes through our SAAS HR software." Sounds pretty good, right? I would say that's an average elevator speech that could be used with phone calls, emails, or text messages.

However, what about this option?

Example two: "Hi Mr. Customer. The reason for my call is because I did some research, and I understand that many companies in your industry are under extreme pressure to automate their HR processes to eliminate human error and avoid costly compliance and privacy penalties."

Which one do you think is more valuable to the customer and will immediately grab their attention? Number two. Sellers who show up as salespeople no longer win at sales. There are too many salespeople who reach out to prospects looking to sell their solution instead of helping customers solve their problems. Customers don't want to spend time with salespeople. They spend their time with trusted advisors and consultants who help them solve their problems.

This is similar to the medical field. Would you ever feel comfortable going to see someone without a formal medical education and practice to diagnose your health symptoms? Likely not. Then why would your customers want to spend time with you if you don't understand their business?

In my career, I've witnessed many sellers make very generalized sales calls. Most of the time when they call, it's like the first example I provided regarding the HR SAAS software. The message isn't terrible, but that customer is receiving so many phone calls from other salespeople saying the exact same thing. You have to find a way to stand out.

Most of the time, these salespeople are able to reach low-level decision-makers in an organization. The barrier to entry is lower, so they don't need to be as strategic with their messaging. They're able to get to managers who may be able to make smaller purchases, but ultimately, they're not the key decision-makers in the organization. Your most difficult and hard to reach prospects are the prospects who will pay you the most. In order to get time with them, you must show up differently than your competitors. Show them that you understand their business and provide a clear and concise message as to why they should take time out of their busy day to meet with you.

If you realize that you're interrupting every prospect that

you reach out to, whether it be phone, email, or text message, you'll start to realize that you need to be valuable in that conversation regarding the business problem that you're trying to help them solve. You must see the bigger picture along with the intricate details of the business problems at hand, either for the company, the industry, or even better, the person.

Now you may be thinking, "Erik, in the previous chapter, you focused on taking immediate action and stomping fear." I did say that, but I also mentioned how important it is for you to do research during non-business hours to make the best use of your time. You have to educate yourself.

Let me ask you this. Is your goal to make as many phone calls as possible or is it to get as many appointments with your prospects as possible so that you can engage in valuable business dialogue with them? I know that my goal has always been to meet with as many customers as I can, not make the most calls. Keep the main thing the main thing.

In the end, you have to do both—take massive action and become very educated in the problems your prospects are trying to solve and how they're going about solving those problems. It's unacceptable to be an uneducated seller. If you desire to earn well above a six-figure income, it's an absolute must. If you're young and competing against more tenured senior sellers, the fastest way to overcome that challenge and gain the respect of your prospects is by becoming extremely informed on their business issues by increasing your business acumen.

In the upcoming chapters, I will share ways to do customer and competitor research. Regardless of whether or not you're given information by your organization, you still need to become well-informed on your own in order to hold a value-added business conversation with your prospects. There is a plethora of free tools available to you: Google, YouTube, the Wall Street Journal, podcasts, and many more right at your fingertips. There's no excuse for not leveraging these easy-to-use tools that are at everyone's disposal.

Most sellers spend less than 5% of their time on self-education. In fact, I would say most do little to none at all. How much time do you currently spend? Are you reading one business-related publication or watching one educational video on your prospect's business or industry every day? If not, it's time to start.

If you're doing none at all, this is the perfect time to start. Add one scheduled self-education activity per day, and you'll be 1% better each and every day. If you're already focused on improving your business acumen through education, keep striving to learn more about your prospect's industry and the ways you can help them.

Self-Education

There are several types of self-education I encourage you to practice. I break these down into four sections.

1. Industry research. What problems are business leaders in the market you serve trying to solve?
2. Specific prospect research. How does your prospect make money? How was their last year of company financial performance? What does the CEO have to say about their business? Who are your prospect's competitors? What issues is the company facing? What is the company strategy?
3. Foundational business knowledge. Do you understand how to read financial statements and where to find them? Do you know the different types of corporations, S Corp, LLC for example? Do you know what an article of incorporation is? Business communications: how do companies communicate and what mediums do they use? Who is involved in business decisions when a company goes to market to make a purchase?
4. Listen. One of the best ways to increase your business acumen is to simply listen. Listen to your prospects and engage with those that are below the decision making level to understand how the company operates. Those that are at an individual producer level or at a line manager level have lower barriers to entry. They're more likely to talk to you, and it allows you to ask great questions to better understand how the business operates, how they make decisions, and who's involved. Listen to your mentors and more talented salespeople in your inner circle. I've found throughout my career that when I spend the most time with my leaders and my mentors, that's when I'm at the top of my game. You should do the same.

You also have the opportunity to engage in networking events with those that are at the top of your industry or niche. Not sure where to find them? As I stated before, Google is your best friend. Don't make it difficult. If you don't have a mentor, it's time to get one. It's one of the best ways to improve your business acumen. You're looking for how they speak, how do they articulate their thoughts in a concise manner? How do they talk about business? Ask them, where do they get their information? Copy what they do, rinse and repeat over and over again. Don't reinvent the wheel.

You are the product of the five closest people you spend your time with. If you spend all your time hanging out with your buddies who aren't business professionals at the top of their game, how do you expect to change? You'll continue to talk the way they talk, spend your time the way they spend their time, and things will never get better.

Moving forward, if you wish to earn the income of your dreams, you must develop business acumen. Start investing in yourself today. You're already taking action and investing in yourself by reading this book. Make sure you also take the time to educate yourself on what your customers care about and drastically improve your prospecting efforts and the number of deals you close.

3

THE SALES CAMPAIGN

This book is based on years and years of experience in the way that I prospect in the B2B sales industry. While I've spent a majority of my career selling IT consulting services, I would apply a similar approach to any industry. Frankly, I may even approach a B2C market in the same fashion. Let me explain why.

Too often, I see social media marketers and online sales coaches providing advice to eager sales reps to go after one lead after another. This tactic does not value building a relationship with the customer. Instead, it's about finding people who are ready to buy immediately. With this strategy, if the prospect is not ready to buy right away, you move on. In my opinion, there is a major flaw in this method and approach, especially in the B2B industry.

Focus on Relationships

When you are prospecting new accounts, it's critical that you understand prospects are not often immediately ready to buy. I'm not saying that you shouldn't be assertive. I'm not saying that you shouldn't be extremely active. I am definitely a proponent of all of those things in the right ways, but what I am suggesting is that you need to look at your customers the same way that you would look at a relationship in your personal life.

For example, it's unlikely that you would take a person out on a date and then ask them to marry you after spending just a few hours with them. Sure, you may have had some customers throughout your career who have agreed to start doing business with you right on the spot. But that's generally not the case.

Human psychology is extremely complex, but there is one thing we could likely all agree on. People take their time in business and personal relationships and are cautious at first. As trust is established and value created for the other person, we become more interested in engaging in exclusive relationships. Knowing that, why is it that we treat prospects and target customers differently?

What I've witnessed throughout my career with newer sales reps and occasionally more senior sellers attempting to get out of a slump is they really don't build any type of sales campaign.

Sales campaigns can be defined as many different things, but typically, it's your marketing approach, the specific customers you're going after, the sales message, what your value proposition is, what your differentiators are, and how you're going to go ahead and attack that market to close business and hit your goals.

The Purpose Behind Pre-Work

How can you develop a strong sales campaign if you haven't done any pre-work to know who your customer is? Take the time to answer the following questions as you begin building your sales campaign:

- How would you describe your perfect customer?
- What problems and major trends in the industry are they trying to solve?
- What problems do you solve?
- Why do you want to do business with them?
- What competitors exist in your market?
- What competitors do they already do business with?
- Are you really the right fit for them?

Newer sellers typically build a list of prospects they want to call. They have prospects A, B, C, and D, and they plan to call these specific accounts over the course of a week. They call each prospect a few times that week, but then they never call again or wait several months before contacting those prospects again.

This can be a huge detriment to your success in sales prospecting because you lose the momentum you build in a sales campaign. Prospects are extremely busy. They are inundated with calls from sellers on a daily basis. Their job is not to take calls from salespeople. Their job is to execute whatever it is that their role and title involves.

If their job is in IT, their role might be leading a large team that builds and architects an IT system. If your prospect works for a company that manufactures something that requires steel, and they are the head of manufacturing, their job encompasses numerous responsibilities. Procuring steel for the operation may only be 10-15% of their job. If your prospect is in procurement, they are likely responsible for cost optimization and building better processes for procuring products and services. On a smaller scale, a restaurant owner's job is to get customers in the door to sell more meals to turn a profit. They are not waiting around for your call. So, you need to have a plan to contact them, gain their

ERIK FISHER

attention, and build a relationship in the long run. Simply put, you must cut through the noise.

The most efficient way to accelerate the achievement of your sales goals and ultimately reach financial freedom is to strategically attack your market with a true sales campaign.

A sales campaign holds many definitions and is applied differently depending on the person and organization. To me, a sales campaign is researching, planning, and executing against a specific plan consistently over time.

After many years in sales, I started paying more attention to the approach I took with my prospecting efforts. I've been selling to Fortune 200 companies for the last twelve years. In nearly every account, I've been able to reach C-Level or VP stakeholders, establish a relationship, provide value, and over time deliver significant outcomes, which has equated to millions of dollars in profit for my company.

Make Repeated Contact

You need to be everywhere your prospects are all the time. They need to think of you when they're looking to solve a problem because you've established credibility and a level of rapport with them. They see you as someone who adds value to their work. Most of your competitors are leveraging the "spray and pray" method, where they make fifty calls during the week to a certain set of prospects. Then they don't call them again for months.

If you don't connect with their concerns, you are forgotten the minute you leave a voicemail. That prospect will not remember you. The only way they're going to remember you is if you've done your homework ahead of time. You know what problems they're trying to solve, so your message lands with them, whether it's through voicemail, email, or social media. It comes across as extremely valuable. They see you as an expert in your industry.

Furthermore, every time they pick up their voicemail and listen to their messages, they need to keep hearing your name. When calling on a specific set of accounts, do so on a rotational basis. Call a certain number of people in and around the prospects you're trying to get in front of, so you have omnipresence. Be everywhere your prospects are. If they go to networking events, you need to be there. If they're working with specific competitors, learn everything you can about what those competitors offer. Talk to people at the ground level and understand why the potential buyer likes working with that particular company.

The point of this is, you need to have multiple touches and multiple attempts over a period of time. This may seem rather obvious to you; however, the execution of this concept and strategy is missed by most sales professionals, leaving them feeling paralyzed wondering why they can't fill their calendar with meetings and a fat pipeline of new business. You don't build a personal relationship, whether it be a friendship or even a love interest, after your first date. Typically, you'll go on multiple dates over the course of maybe six months to a year, and in my case, multiple years, before you find out that person is the right person for you and vice versa. You need to look at your customers and prospects the same way.

You're building momentum every time you reach out to that particular prospect and have a conversation with them. They respond to an email. There is a social media touch. Every single attempt at contact and actual conversation or face-to-face meeting is moving you closer to your goal of getting that customer to want to buy from you when they have a business problem they're trying to solve. If you try to attack your accounts and your territory, always trying to close a deal with whatever prospect you're talking to, you're going to come across very transactional, and your customers will see right through you.

Often, when I ask my current customers why they do business with me, they say it's because I build meaningful relationships with them. I take the time to understand their business. I'm not trying too hard to close them just for the sake of making a sale.

You start seeing massive results over time when you have focused effort over a consistent period of time and invest in relationships with your customers, understand what they're trying to solve, and bring value to the table. This can take time.

Yes, you need to have a lengthy hit list or lead list. You can't have a short runway because, eventually, you'll only have so many people to call. I would never argue with that. However, once you have your set of accounts and prospects that you are going to target for that quarter or for that year, build a plan that includes how often you're going to reach out to those people. As you build your plan, answer the following questions:

- What's your message?
- What will your communication be?
- What's the value proposition you're going to provide?
- What kind of free value are you going to provide?
- How are you going to catch their attention differently than your competitors?
- How are you going to repeat that and add massive value over and over again each and every time you reach out to that person?
- How are you going to leverage the multiple channels and communication mediums available to you, so that you're not consistently reaching out the same way every time?

- How are you going to be everywhere your customer is and become omnipresent?

Ultimately, your goal is to court your prospects to the point that, when they are ready to solve a business problem, you and your organization come to mind first. If you take this approach throughout your sales career, you will not only build meaningful relationships, which you and your customers will gain a lot of intrinsic value from, but you'll also massively grow your business. You will maintain customers for a longer period of time because they know that you have their best interests in mind.

Building and executing a sales campaign for my prospective customers has been one of the greatest factors that has allowed me to experience amazing success in sales over the last fifteen years. I've always played the long game and sought out meaningful relationships while adding value. You have the ability to do the same. You just have to do your homework as described in this book, so that you can prospect like a pro.

4

READY, AIM, FIRE: DEFINING YOUR PERFECT CUSTOMER

This chapter will be a bit unconventional compared to most sales books in that we will work through some exercises to help you build your sales campaign through understanding your company, your perfect customer, their personas, your competition, and how to segment your accounts to make the best use of your prospecting efforts and leverage your most valuable asset: time. As a result, you will have a fully functioning sales campaign you can implement right away.

As we begin building our sales campaign, it makes sense to talk about the most important part of the equation: the customer. But before we do that, we need to understand ourselves. What is our company's vision? What is our *why*? What problems do we solve and for whom? If we better understand ourselves, we can make more calculated decisions as we build our sales campaign.

Defining Your Perfect Customer

Before you can begin customer outreach, you need to have a good grasp on who your ideal customer is and who they are not. This will vary from business to business and your product or service. In order to attract the right customers to meet with you or buy from you, it's critical that you do some pre-work to define important criteria that will help make your prospecting efforts more targeted.

Begin by thinking about a few questions:

- What industry, market, niche, or department do they serve?
- What are the major problems your customers face?
- What are the different titles or labels your customer uses to define themselves?

Please complete the exercises in the *Ready. Aim. Fire Workbook* to help you define your perfect customer.

Your Customer Persona

Let's go a step deeper. I'd like you to go into as much detail as possible to define the roles, job titles, and labels your customers and/or their companies refer to them by. This is a critical step as it will help you identify the right prospects to reach out to via the Multiple Communication Medium Framework (MCMF), which will be introduced in Chapter 9.

For example, if you were selling cybersecurity software, your customer titles may include Chief Information Officer (CIO), Chief Information Security Officer (CISO), Vice President of Security, VP of Security, Chief Risk Officer, Director of Data Protection, Director of Security Engineering, Manager of Threat Intelligence, and Security Architect.

I encourage you to use Google, LinkedIn, Facebook, Twitter, friends, and colleagues to gain as much information as you go through the exercise in the workbook. Get creative and take some time to think about the various ways your perfect customer may label themselves.

For large enterprise companies, there are likely many different roles and titles used by potential customers. For a mid-market or small business (SMB), there will be fewer people in the organization, so fewer titles. This is where you need to use your creativity and imagination as the title or labels will be broader and less defined in nature.

Using my example above for security software, an SMB may not have a Chief Security Officer but they likely have a CIO or VP of IT, or possibly the company has no IT leadership and only a CEO. These titles don't fall within the traditional naming conventions used by our target buyer; however, this is where great customer opportunities can be overlooked. If you are overlooking these potential buyers, perhaps so is your competition, and the opportunity is ripe for the picking. Conversely, keep in mind that this type of customer may also fall outside the criteria you define in the third exercise in the *Ready. Aim. Fire Workbook.*

Once you've defined the possible naming conventions your perfect customer identifies with, refine your description even further and be SPECIFIC. With that said, be only as specific as required for your product or service. For example, if you serve financial services clients including all financial services sub-niches such as insurance, then there is no need to narrow further. However, if you serve only trading clients, it's critical that you define your target customer precisely. This is important for future steps of your sales campaign. The more targeted you can be with your outreach, your message, value creation, and vision, the more success you'll see in your efforts.

Use the bulleted items below as a reference point. Whether you know the answers to these or not today is not important. Be resourceful and find the answer. You may serve multiple different markets, so it's perfectly acceptable to list a broader range, but keep in mind that we are looking for our perfect customer scenario.

- Market, Sector or Vertical
- Geography: Continent, Country, Region, State, County, Territory Lines
- Revenue Criteria: < $1,000,000, $5M-$15M, $15-$50M, $50M-$100M, $1B-$5B etc.
- Total Employees
- Public, Private, Start-Up
- Years in Business
- Workers in Department
- Technology and Equipment Requirements
- Compliance and Regulatory Requirements

The criteria you establish is a general guide, nothing more and nothing less. You still have to do the work and consistently refine your criteria over time.

Please keep in mind that if you are selling to a geographic territory or region, it may not be necessary or possible to narrow the criteria using all the suggested bullets. That's okay! This is sales after all, so while you need to be precise in knowing who and what you're going after, in some cases, your prospecting efforts will help you define this through the feedback and data you collect through trial and error. Don't make the mistake of only going after the big fish as there is plenty of revenue in the SMB market with less red tape. You just may need more customers in total to reach your goals.

The biggest complaint I hear from new salespeople is, "My territory stinks!" or "I need more leads!" The truth is they haven't begun prospecting intentionally with enough effort to make that claim.

Spending your time on the right prospects is imperative to shortening your prospecting cycle time to convert prospects into customers. We invest time upfront on this effort for a reason. *Everyone* is not your customer. As a salesperson, our time is extremely valuable. The wrong clients can be a massive time suck; even the right clients will suck away your precious time if you allow them to. Let your real-world feedback and data guide you as you refine your perfect customer further, but keep an open mind as there could be a diamond in the rough you'll miss if you put blinders on.

Segmentation and List Building

As you worked through the exercises, you may have felt that it was labor-intensive and overly detailed. Perhaps you felt that it was a waste of time. I can understand and relate. Sure, it may seem that stepping up to bat with no strategy and swinging away could result in a few home runs; it may even work for a small subset of the population. However, in today's economy with the enhanced sophistication of our target buyers, that's not the best strategy if you're looking for long-term, sustainable growth.

The real question is, how do we balance quality and quantity? Whether you have just started your sales career or have been in the game for some time, you understand that you will need a high volume of outreach activity in order to succeed in sales. How and where we spend our time becomes incredibly important. We want to show up in our best form with companies we want to do business with the most based on the data we collected that shows the potential for the most opportunity. They deserve the majority of our time, but they also deserve our best effort when our skills are peaking.

The best approach to tackle this is by segmenting our territory or market into three segments.

Tier 1, Tier 2, and Tier 3 accounts:

- Tier 1 accounts are defined by companies that

meet all of our major and minor perfect customer requirements. These are usually easily defined as our largest opportunities for growth as there is significant data that validates why we should focus our prime efforts and attention on these companies. Typically, salespeople have no problem identifying these companies, as there is a plethora of evidence that suggests these companies could be a major growth lever.

- Tier 2 accounts are defined by companies that meet two-thirds of our perfect customer criteria. These accounts are companies that meet our industry and revenue requirements, but we also have data to back up the fact that we know they invest money in the product or services we provide. They may be lacking in employee headcount, number of locations, or other ancillary requirements. This could be a larger mid-market company that deserves attention but isn't an A-grade target based on the prior pre-work you completed.

- Tier 3 accounts are defined by companies that meet one-third of our perfect customer criteria. Perhaps they are in the industry we serve, but they are on the lowest end of revenue and employee headcount. These companies aren't necessarily small, but they could have major barriers to entry, small budgets, or complicated funding and buying cycles that may not be worth our time based on our pre-work.

Once you have evaluated and segmented your territory, it is time to build your hit list based on your pre-work, the personas and labels that your perfect customers use. The best approach is to take each of the accounts in each tier and work through them by identifying each prospect with the identified persona and label that could be potential decision-makers or influencers and add them to your list in your CRM or spreadsheet. LinkedIn Sales Navigator, Data.com, Seamless.ai, ZoomInfo, and many other SAAS-based tools are great for building your list and identifying prospects within your three tiers. If you don't have funding or access to the paid tools, LinkedIn's basic plan is free and can get the job done in helping you identify the prospects to build your lists.

The Power Hour

Most people can only focus for short periods of time. The main issues I see consistently with most salespeople is that their prospecting efforts aren't targeted with specifically tailored messages to each prospect and they just sprinkle calls throughout the day. Like most things in life that we strive to improve in, it's important to get into a rhythm and build momentum. One of the most effective ways to do this is to create one-hour power blocks of time to focus on your sales outreach activity.

Now that you have built your prospecting hit list, the best approach to prospect most effectively is to start each prospecting power hour with your Tier 3 accounts. Why? I don't know about you, but no matter how long I've been selling, much like an athlete, I need some time to warm up. Athletes practice 90% of their careers and only play in games or matches the other 10%. That's an incredible advantage to reach peak performance. As salespeople, we are in the game 100% of the time. The last thing we want to do is make a poor sales call when we aren't warmed up, primed, and in the flow of our sales calls.

With that in mind, I suggest starting your sales call blocks with your lowest priority targets, your Tier 3 segment. You will make mistakes and stumble and freeze when you run into objections. We all do. With Tier 3 accounts, it doesn't matter. These companies have low ROI potential, and you are essentially using them to warm up your brain and prime it for your Tier 2 and Tier 1 accounts. Throughout your power hour, start with a determined list of Tier 3 contacts and work your way up to your Tier 1 accounts, where you'll spend 50% of your focused block of time.

While it's critical to just get moving and start taking action in sales, aiming for the wrong target with the wrong message can result in spinning your wheels and lead to massive frustration. I've been there. Prospecting is hard enough without making it more difficult on ourselves. When you know your audience and their problems, you're better able to relate to them in your sales message and dive deeper into their pains, problems, and goals.

With the fierce competitive landscape we all face, it is more important now than ever to know who you are targeting in your outreach and, equally important, why you are targeting them. What problems do you help solve?

Knowing your target audience allows you to maximize each attempted contact through a laser-focused sales message that cuts through the noise like a hot butter knife. There is no better feeling than knowing your audience so incredibly well that prospecting becomes fun and easy!

Most of your peers and competitors are not engaged in the level of detail outlined in this book. If you want to be great at sales, you need to do the things others aren't willing to do. When you master your skills in reaching your audience, you will engage in more prospecting activity, which will lead to a fuller funnel and sales quotas you blow past quarter after quarter.

5

GOING ABOVE THE POWER BAND

W here I've been most successful in my career is getting to key decision-makers faster. Most sales reps in any industry struggle with not talking to decision-makers. When you're not talking to decision-makers, it slows down all deals. There's a saying: "Time kills all deals." The longer a deal is out there, the quicker it dies because there's something you didn't uncover during the discovery phase that prevents the deal from getting done. Additionally, true decision-makers typically carry a very different lens than those lower in rank in the organization. They are responsible for taking a more strategic approach.

Often in a B2B sales pursuit, there are several stakeholders involved in the purchasing process. While you may believe you're working with a decision-maker, often you're not, which is uncovered when your deal stalls, doesn't close at all, or worse yet, you lose to a competitor that completely caught you off guard. I've come out the other side of these situations a loser many times throughout my career. Almost every time, it was because I wasn't talking to an executive-level decision-maker. In large enterprises, these personas are often vice presidents or possibly C-level executives. In a small to medium-sized business, maybe it's the owner of the company or someone holding the title of director.

Ultimately, you need to find people who can sign the check and have both the power and influence to make big decisions for the good of the organization without needing anyone else's approval. Beyond that, executives see the bigger picture for the organization. The good news for us is that big picture items are often more simplistic. I like simple. When you connect with this level of decision-maker, the entire sales game changes. It's what separates the mediocre from the elite. This is what I call going above the power band.

While it may seem obviously important to spend time prospecting senior-level executives, the truth is that very few sales reps do it at all. Why is it that we don't do the things we know will undoubtedly help our business? In my experience, it's because it's both extremely challenging and intimidating, so fear creeps in and no action is taken at all. How can you accomplish that feat when you have had no luck so far or are incredibly fearful of reaching out to an executive? Do your research and have very tailored messages. This will help reduce the number of attempts you need to make in order to get in front of key decision-makers faster.

Accelerating Sales with Decision Makers

When you're in a business-to-business sales environment, you want to do everything you can to accelerate your sales cycle. In B2B, our sales cycles are longer to begin with as deals can be more complex, larger in total volume or revenue, and usually involve multiple decision-makers. Everything accelerates when you're dealing with a true decision-maker versus someone who acts like a decision-maker. When it comes to prospecting and staying sticky with your customer throughout a sales cycle, your sales closing rate will accelerate drastically when you stay consistent with the methods outlined in this book. Just as important, you want your product or service to solve business problems. If you are not connected with the overarching business problem that an executive cares about, the chances of your deal being killed when it goes to get signed off on are more likely.

At the end of the day, executives have the ability to move money and override the decisions of others. If you're not working with people who have the ability to control budgets and move money, you're dealing with influencers in the decision-making process, but not the final, true decision-makers. Therefore, the process itself is going to take longer because you don't have all the information nor the proper alignment and relationships.

Connecting with Decision Makers

If you want to know if you are working with a true decision-maker, just ask the question. It is an appropriate question to ask as you move through the sales process. The question could come up during your first meeting with a prospect where you're engaged in the discovery process or perhaps later depending on flow of the conversation and trust level that you've established.

When it comes to finding out if the person's a true decision-maker, you simply could ask, "Who else needs to be involved in the decision for this product or service?" Oftentimes, they will say, "It's me and a few of my partners."

You then want to ask follow up questions. At a certain spend threshold, there is usually an executive that needs to sign off on the purchase. As an example, you could say, "Typically for a company of this size, you're looking at somewhere in the $700,000 to a million-dollar range for our product or service. Are you able to make that decision or do we need to invite other people to the conversation?" Alternatively, you could ask, "When you purchased something like this in the past, what's the decision-making process, and who else was involved?" Often, the response from the prospect will be, "Once we believe this is the right fit, I might invite a couple of other internal partners to the table. From there, if we identify that we do want to do business with you, we will pull in our purchasing and legal departments."

Keep asking questions about the process until you find out who ultimately signs off on the deal.

Just ask the prospect to walk you through what that looks like. Nothing more complicated than that. If they're the decision-maker, they will tell you that they sign off on engagements like this all the time. They don't need to seek approval from anybody else, and they won't hesitate to let you know.

Selling to the Top

If you start your prospecting efforts focused at the top of the organization or department, you're focused on reaching a final decision-maker. If you're starting with a president, vice president, C-level executive, CFO, chief marketing officer, or CEO, you already know you're at the top of the list.

At this juncture, if you are working with an executive, they will likely direct you downstream to someone on their staff who will handle the operations of the deal. When it comes to the actual decision, they're going to go back up to the top anyway. Wouldn't it be nice to already be connected to the executive-level decision-maker and have the ability to go back to them when it's time to close the deal? Of course, it would!

At the end of the day, when you identify who the decision-makers are above the power band that you're going to target in your prospecting, they're ultimately going to delegate you downwards below the power band to someone on their team. However, once you go down, you always can go back up. If you start down below the power band, it's much harder to go up than it is to go back down.

Identify the Personas of Your Target Customer

If you sell marketing services to an SMB, you know that most of those companies don't have a chief marketing officer. However, they may have a marketing director or a director of marketing and sales.

Reach out to the president of the company and say, "We offer SEO or marketing services for companies that are in the food and beverage industry, and we work with X, Y, Z customers in your industry and help them achieve a three times revenue growth over the course of 12 months. We'd like to spend some time with you to understand what your objectives are and talk to you about how we can help you." If you're talking to a president, you would ask, "Are you the appropriate person to talk to about that?" They might say, "Actually yes, ultimately, I am the decision-maker for that. But the person who handles that more at a technical level or at a more detailed level is my chief marketing officer or the director of marketing for my company."

What you shouldn't do is call or email an executive and say, "Can you help me understand who the right person to talk to about this is?" That's extremely general and a waste of their time.

In this day and age, it's frankly unacceptable to not know who your target persona is for the product or service that you're selling. We have social platforms that you can use to research and find out who you need to contact.

Ask for Permission

If the vice president tells you the director of marketing handles purchasing decisions for your product or service, you might be okay going and talking with the director of marketing, working out the details, and then personally going back to the VP, rather than letting the marketing director go to the VP.

While the VP may direct you down to the chief marketing officer, you can still ask them what key priorities they are trying to achieve via their marketing investments. Let them know you want to make sure you are addressing their business objectives and ask if you can reach out to them with any questions you have. They're likely going to say yes. They don't want the company to spend time with you if you're not going to address their business problems.

If you do not ask for permission and set up a communication plan this way, then the other person you are working with may feel you are going over their head when you communicate with the VP in the future. From the start, let the person you are working with know that the VP has encouraged you to communicate with him to ensure that the company's business objectives are being met.

Be Specific

In my experience, most people are extremely uncomfortable calling executives because they don't know what to say. Unfortunately, that hinders their ability to get wildly successful very quickly. Oftentimes, they overcomplicate it. When someone doesn't know what to say and they're worried, they just send emails using untailored, generic communication to executives. They use the "spray and pray" method, which does not work. Those emails are just going to end up in prospect's spam or email trash.

If you want to get sticky with executives, you need to do a little bit of research on who your target personas are, but when you're messaging these people, try not to overcomplicate it. What are the biggest challenges in their industry? What problems or initiatives is their company trying to solve? What business cycle is their company or department in that is relevant to your product or service? Are there any transformational changes happening in their company or industry? Take that information and look for stories of other people that you've already helped solve a similar business problem or of other companies that are going through a similar challenge that your product/services solves.

After you've completed your research, grab their attention with a specifically tailored message by leveraging the intelligence you gathered. A laser-focused message will catch their attention and generate more interest than the generalized messages your competitors are sending.

Typically, it's going to take consistent application of a sales cadence to catch the attention of the executive. So, don't give up when you don't receive a response back via email or are unable to reach them by phone. Executives are busy people. The fact that it's difficult to reach them is intentional. Only the best salespeople will make contact.

While you may get lucky and reach the executive the first try, more than likely, it's going to be an email, a phone call, and a LinkedIn message repeated several different times over the course of weeks or months where you're providing valuable and insightful information. In some cases, it's taken me a year to make contact with an executive-level decision-maker.

I once witnessed a panel interview of several C-level executives. In the interview, they were asked about vendor emails. All the executives stated that generic mass-marketed emails are automatically deleted or ignored. However, the ones they do answer are specifically tailored to their industry or their company.

And to be specific, these are not book-long emails. An executive doesn't have hours to read an email. They have thirty seconds to look at their phone. If you're sending a cold email to an executive, create a catchy subject line that speaks to the business problems they're going through. In the first three sentences, they know who you are, what you do, what business problems you solve, and how that impacts them. It's that simple.

Don't Be Intimidated

A lot of salespeople are very young, yet they're paid to call men or women twice their age with advanced degrees responsible for running multi-million dollar budgets. It's understandably intimidating; however, it doesn't need to be that way. Often, they overcomplicate the fact that the prospects they are intimidated by are just people. All they needed to do was a little bit of research that shows how they're different from all their competitors. Remember, all you're asking for is their time. Once you get their time, you go into discovery mode to understand more about what they care about.

If you want to become a successful seller who earns the top 1% in your industry, you need to sell to the top. Realize that it's going to take some effort and it's not going to happen overnight. The only way to make it happen is to force yourself to get comfortable calling above the power band.

You have to show up properly because you don't get a million chances. If you bug an executive over and over, and your message is not tailored to them or their industry, you might get yourself completely ignored by that company forever. You have to do it in a way that's meaningful and impactful to them and their business because they don't have a lot of time.

If you're not dealing with decision-makers, you're just lengthening the process to get an answer. Ultimately, you want your product or service tied to the highest-ranking executive's priorities every time. If it's not a priority for an executive, it's unimportant to the company. Doesn't mean you won't sell it. It just means you're probably not going to expand much.

If you want to get sticky with your customers, everything you do should be tied to an overall business objective. Whether it's a solution, a service, or a product, those are the deals that don't die because it's tied to a primary business objective.

The ones that aren't tied to that are the ones that lose funding. You think it's important, but it really isn't. It might be important to someone who says they're a decision-maker, but they're not. So you waste a lot of time.

When you're tied to an executive, the whole process gets easier for you. It requires a little more upfront work, but sales get a lot easier because you don't have to try to convince people who aren't decision-makers to do business with you because their boss is telling them that they should.

Like most salespeople, I wasn't calling executives when I first got into business-to-business sales. It's scary. When you're younger, you're not as confident. People who are older usually aren't as afraid of calling executives. When you're 25 years old, it's intimidating to call someone who's 60 years old and running a $500 million business.

I quickly improved my messaging with people who were right on the cusp of that power band, and I got very, very specific. I learned how to use intelligence, information, and data to craft extremely quality messages. Once I did this, my results skyrocketed. A lot of people are sitting there banging away and making a thousand calls, and I was able to do far more than they were with more strategic effort.

Everything I was doing was very focused on a few things:

- Who are they?
- What do they care about?
- How can I help them solve that problem?
- Why would they read this email or listen to my voicemail?
- Why would they call me back?

After a few years in B2B sales, I began experiencing success, but not to the level I hoped to achieve. I realized that if I wanted to advance my career to the next level, I needed to stop being afraid of calling executives.

I'm in the IT consulting industry, so a lot of the people at the management and director level are very technical. But the leaders who actually sign checks for large deals are not as technical. It is actually easier for me to have a conversation with them.

I just found that as long as the message you craft is specific and tailored to them, you can open doors very quickly. It forced the people a notch below the power band, the people I always struggled to get in front of in the first place, to work with me. They ignore you all the time because they're getting hammered by salespeople. There's less noise from salespeople above the power band. When decision-makers would tell those people to work with me, the whole process got easier.

For one particular company I worked with over the course of seven years, I started with lower-level people, built relationships, and made some transactional sales. Once I really understood what was happening inside the organization, I started calling on the executive, who had a tremendous amount of power and influence. By working directly with him, I was able to quickly line up multiple deals. I had to do a lot of work because any deal that's worth seven figures is going to require a lot of effort.

However, the struggle for most salespeople is not the close. It's really all about the prospecting and the lead-up, setting yourself up so that there is no close at all. They're going to do business with you because you understand what they're trying to accomplish. You can tie everything that you learned by working with those executives back to whatever your product or service is. As long as those things align and you have a pretty good grasp on what their budget is, your results will go through the roof.

If you're working with an executive, you're going to know what those top priorities are. Someone below the power band may have different priorities than an executive. Everybody has a different set of priorities. It just makes sense to understand what the priorities are at the top. That's where all the bigger deals are going to be.

The head of the company is leading the company to where it needs to go. The people in the middle or down at the bottom may not even know what those goals are or where things are going because they're so stuck in the day to day of just trying to manage their responsibilities and direct reports.

If you sell office supplies, you could sell those to different departments within a school district and work with one or two schools. But what if you were selling to the superintendent of the school district? Odds are probably in your favor that you're going to be able to sell to the entire school district versus just a couple of schools.

If you're selling software and you're only focused on one specific department within an organization, you're limiting yourself. If you were selling to someone above the power band, they could direct you to a list of potential customers within their organization, opening up significant opportunities you may not have known existed. To state that people below the power band don't have the ability to make their own buying decisions would be completely untrue. I've developed great relationships with customers below the power band over the years and have sold many services to these customers. In fact, the best leaders at my customers show strong leadership in trusting in their direct reports' supplier relationships and corresponding buying decisions, to a certain point.

With that said, you must do both—call above and below the power band. When selling to decision-makers above the power band, your ability to make a bigger impact on your prospect's and customer's strategic business priorities grow. Alignment to strategic priorities can equate to a more streamlined sales cycle, less friction, and the ability to grab a larger piece of opportunity and revenue for you and your organization.

The Answer is Above the Power Band

When prospecting, it can be difficult to assess the prospective company's goals when working below the power band. Often, it is only the executives who know the company's bigger goals and vision. Working above the power band can save you time by helping you quickly determine if your product or service fits their needs.

I got advice from a very successful salesperson during my first year in B2B sales. I probably had six years of sales under my belt at the time, but it was all B2C up until that point. I asked him, "What's your secret to success?" He asked me, "How much money do you want to make?" I told him I wanted to be a millionaire. He did the math for me real quick and told me my time is worth $800 an hour. While I'm not paid hourly, time and currency are how every deal is consumed.

I thought to myself, if I was going to spend eight hours a week focusing on a customer who was never going to buy from me because my product or service doesn't fit into them, I was basically wasting $800 for every hour I spent on that company. That always stuck with me. Once I learned to sell to executives, I began to understand what *they* cared about. Once I understood what they cared about, I tailored all my messaging to the most important priorities in the business, which were bigger picture items that not only resonated well with the executive stakeholders but were topics I was much more comfortable discussing.

It also allowed me to quickly disqualify people I didn't want to spend my time with. Then I could focus on the next prospect or prospective company.

A few years ago, a young man at our company was given a Fortune 100 company, one of the largest companies in the world. He had a problem though. He kept getting stuck with non-decision makers. He'd have a few meetings and then they would become non-responsive.

I sat him down and asked him why he thought the prospect wasn't getting back to him. He told me he didn't know. I let him know there could be a couple of different reasons.

If a prospect is not getting back to you, it is possible that your conversation didn't add enough value or help them understand how your product or service can solve their problem. Maybe the problem isn't that important to them. Another possibility is that they are busy executing on other priorities. Ultimately, whatever they spend their time on is what their leaders are telling them to spend their time on.

We started looking at the personas within that specific area of this large account. We had not done business in this particular area for a number of years, and all the leadership had changed. We crafted a very compelling message, and he was able to set up a meeting with a senior executive vice president within one attempt.

From working above the power band, we were able to better understand the executive's vision and determine that our product or service didn't fit into his model. It became very apparent that what he was pitching and selling was not a priority for the executives. A tremendous amount of time could have been wasted talking to people below the power band. Through targeted, tailored messaging, he was able to get in front of an executive at a very young age. Because he did the necessary upfront research and spoke to what was important to that executive, he was able to get an hour of his time and then prevent himself from wasting an exorbitant amount of time on an attractive target customer that wasn't a fit.

All salespeople want a success story where they were able to establish a relationship with an executive and have it turn into a life-changing sale that altered the trajectory of their career and life forever. The more likely scenario a lot of people are going to run into is what I just described. They have a better understanding of the vision and the strategy. They can decide if it's the right company to spend their time with, or they'll figure out that they were spending their time with the wrong people and that executive will direct them to the right people who could actually make those decisions.

The best salespeople spend more time disqualifying customers than qualifying customers. Disqualify people so you don't waste your time instead of trying to qualify everybody into whatever it is you sell. The absolute best salespeople choose who they're going to spend time with.

Collecting Intelligence Action Step

Are you ready to take the first steps toward implementing The Intelligence Factor? Go to your *Ready. Aim. Fire Workbook* and complete the exercises and questions for Part I. Within the workbook, you will find exercises to help you define your persona, define your customer's persona, and determine how to segment accounts into tiers.

To access your complimentary *Ready. Aim. Fire Workbook*, go to www.TheIntelligenceFactor.com/freeworkbook

PART II

VALUABLE INSIGHTS

6
_____

THE MOST IMPORTANT FACTORS OF ALL: PROBLEM SOLVING AND VALUE CREATION

Before you begin customer outreach, it's important to cover the most commonly overlooked aspect of selling: Value Creation. Value creation is the nucleus of every deal. Without it, your ability to close customers will suffer. If you do happen to get lucky and land a few sales, the customer will often be left with buyer's remorse, which will impact your ability to sell to them more in the future and scale to new customers.

Too often, sales reps prospect with the goal of selling the other person on buying their product or service or trying to impress them by throwing around figures and stats about how great their company is, which is meaningless at first. People and companies don't buy anything because you are selling it to them. In fact, if you start pitching out of the gates, you do much more harm than good. Most buyers are strongly turned off by those that approach sales prospecting with the primary goal of selling the other person something. Customers typically buy for one reason only: The Desired Outcome.

When Value Isn't Enough

Before I go on, I'd like to throw in a caveat to my own statement that customers only buy for one reason. It's not always 100% true, as many prospects are unwilling to change due to emotional reasons rather than rational decisions. Many times, customers are unwilling to make a change even though they have evidence that proves their current relationship with a person or company isn't yielding the desired result or, in some cases, worsening it. Ever present an offer to a prospect that will undoubtedly improve their current situation and help them reach their desired outcome, yet they are unwilling to make a change? My guess is you've encountered this situation before, and you'll encounter it again.

Unfortunately, there are prospects that see change as "high risk." They'd rather continue making the same bad decisions, spending money that doesn't provide the value they desire because they fear the unknown. They may see change as a complicated drain on their most precious resource: time. In some cases, they are 100% correct. Change can be complicated and scary, but it's important for us as salespeople to identify these prospects early on in our discovery phase to understand if they are our ideal customer.

There are countless other political reasons that prospects may be unwilling to change in the end, even if they desire a better situation than they are currently in. In some cases, you may do everything correctly in your sales process only to lose in the end when you attempt to close the deal. As you continue on in your career, it's important to take note of these experiences, leverage your intuition, and ask better questions early on to prevent yourself from wasting too much time on these types of prospects. You want to work with prospects who are open-minded enough to change, have the political power to change, make rational decisions, and value honest relationships.

Some prospects just need more nurturing over time, which is why I'm such a big proponent of playing the long game in sales.

Have you ever been interested in dating someone who didn't give you the time of day for what seemed like an eternity; however, after nurturing that relationship over time, they came around and you embarked on a loving and valuable relationship? It happens all the time. While I don't encourage wasting time with prospects who aren't a good fit for your business, I do encourage all sales professionals to understand it may take a significant amount of time to acquire a customer. They don't all come around the first, third, or fourth time. Sometimes, your most difficult to acquire customers become your best and biggest customers—the ones you can hang your hat on for years to come.

While there are some prospects unwilling and incapable of making rational decisions, it's important to understand that of all things involved in your sales process, the most important part is creating value for your customers.

Creating Value

Value creation can be defined as your ability to help a prospect solve a problem, gain pleasure, or move away from pain.

Furthermore, in the B2B market, customers typically invest their time and money in exchange for services that help them accomplish four things:
1) Grow Revenue
2) Reduce Risk
3) Increase efficiency/productivity
4) Save Money
Any and all products or services must be tied back to one

or all of these pillars of value creation. If you are unable to describe how your product or service helps your customer accomplish one of these business drivers, you need to think deeply about the bigger picture of how you can help a customer accomplish their business or personal objectives and practice articulating this in a clear and concise manner.

When selling a product or service, one of the most missed opportunities is a salesperson's ability to tie their product or service back to the primary business issue at hand and the value they can provide a prospect. This is critical to our prospecting efforts as we have a very short window of opportunity to catch our prospects' attention. Value is how we do that.

Desired Future State

Typically, as sellers, we get excited and miss the forest for the trees. We believe the problem we are solving is the primary problem, when in reality it's the secondary or surface problem we are solving disguised as the primary problem. The best sellers are able to bridge the gap between the offer and the desired future state.

People buy or invest in products or services that help them realize their desired future state, not those with the most features.

Oftentimes, our customers miss or forget the primary problem they are looking to solve as well. While I focus on the four value pillars as the primary drivers of purchase decisions, which are rational decisions, emotional decision making does come into play even with large enterprises. At the end of the day, humans are still making decisions, and organizations can be highly political. Determining your prospect's rational and emotional factors that go into their decision making becomes a critical part of the sales process during the discovery phase.

Even so, it's best to start with what we know to be true; customers go to market to solve business outcomes and achieve the desired goal. They do not buy features and benefits alone. It's our job to paint the picture for them to show them how we can help them solve their greater business problem or achieve their overall strategic goal. This is a critical step since customers are often attracted to shiny objects and may have a siloed perspective on what options they have to solve their problem or reach their goal.

Through educating our customer and asking great questions combined with anchors, we can help them see alternative options that may have a great impact on the overall goal. Because of this, remember that secondary problems may have great curb appeal, but they don't get sticky with customers. While I'm applying this to a B2B sales scenario, this principle applies to B2C sales scenarios as well. Here are a couple of B2B examples:

Scenario #1

A salesperson sells security software and professional services to implement the software. The large profit is made through the add-on upsell to professional services, which provides software implementation, advisory services, and setting up the clients foundational elements of their security program.

Surface-Level Problem: Prospect has security vulnerabilities in their IT systems and needs to buy security software that identifies vulnerabilities in their IT systems so they can be remediated.

Root Problem: Prospect needs to improve its risk posture to prevent a data breach that will affect the company's shareholders, stock price, and prevent financial penalties. The current security frameworks and controls in place today are immature and require some major upgrades to improve the foundation of their security organization. Without proper up-to-date controls, no matter what software they buy, they will be limited in their ability to govern the software and the decisions of the people in the organization to prevent a cybersecurity breach.

Erik's Two Cents: In this scenario, the buyer is on a mission to find the best in class security software to identify security vulnerabilities as they feel this will solve their problems. While this may seem like the root problem and what the customer believes they need to solve their problem, it may not be exactly what they need to realize value from their investment or purchase. If your company can help them see the bigger picture, then there could be additional products or services you can add on or sell that will help them achieve their overall goal for the future to protect the company.

Perhaps you uncover that they are not the right customer for you at this point. It would be best to nurture the relationship until they are at a point where you can better help them achieve a more measurable valuable outcome. This approach would serve them as your customer as well as you and your business.

Now, if you sell security software, I'm *not* saying that you should run from the opportunity to sell the prospect your software. I am saying to dig deeper, ask better questions about what business problems they are looking to solve, and tie valuable insights into how you can help them achieve their overall goal.

If you ever want to better help your customers achieve their goals while expanding the size of your deals, this is a great way to level up your game.

Scenario #2

Surface-Level Problem: Prospect is looking to buy or lease a larger real estate building for their growing salesforce in an urban setting because they believe that's where the best talent resides to grow their team.

Root Problem: According to the CEO and the company's annual report, the company's operational costs are through the roof along with lagging sales numbers. This problem has created a negative impact on their overall market share due to the inability to make other strategic investments to grow the business in order to stay competitive. If the business is unable to reduce operational costs and grow its sales this year, they will be forced to undergo mass layoffs and potentially file for bankruptcy.

Erik's Two Cents: In this scenario, the salesperson is a Real Estate Banker or Real Estate Agent. The salesperson may feel obligated to show the prospective buyer real estate in the heart of the big urban city. However, this investment will come with a significant rise in operational costs to the prospect, which is already a problem for them. Wise salespeople will look to add more value by offering to better understand the root causes of their problems and overall goals (Reduce Operational Costs, Grow Sales, Strategic Investment Growth). From there, they can share market data and pricing in urban locations paired with talent data for salespeople in geographic areas.

With the value delivered to the client via insights, the salesperson can then show the prospect real estate in a nearby suburban location with train access to the city which solves multiple problems:

1. Access to top talent in the big city = Grow Sales Team = Grow Sales and Market Share
2. Lower Real Estate costs = Lower operational costs
3. Lower Ops Costs + More Sales = More funding for Strategic Investments

If you are selling B2C, here is another example of root

problems vs. surface-level problems. In B2C, consumers may be looking to solve a "problem," but they also buy for other reasons. For example, selling a prospect life insurance doesn't bring someone closer to pleasure; however, it does provide an outcome of providing a prospect with financial security . However, anyone buying a lakehouse property is not solving the same problem as they likely have the financial means to make such a purchase. They also likely have a roof over their head, clothes on their back, and money saved for a rainy day. The prospect looking to purchase a lakefront summer home is seeking pleasure and potentially social status.

Now let's get into an easy and very common example:

Scenario #3

Surface-Level Problem: Prospect is looking to buy a brand new BMW 7 Series as their current sedan is high in mileage, and they need something safer with a great crash rating to protect their family in the event of an accident. They know that BMW's have great features and safety benefits. The 7 Series is a large sedan that solves this problem.

Root Problem: The prospect will likely not disclose this, but the real reason they want a BMW 7 Series is that they see it as a sign of social status, that they've made it in life. In their mind, only those with great financial means can drive a BMW 7 Series. This vehicle will be a status symbol to show their friends, family, and clients that they are well off or perhaps wealthy. Additionally, the neighbor down the street just bought one, and he is the talk of the neighborhood. Everyone envies his car, his lifestyle, and his seemingly amazing life.

Erik's Two Cents: If you know anything about cars, or even if you don't, the BMW 7 Series is no doubt a nice ride, but at a price tag over $100,000, there are plenty of more economical options in the marketplace that offer the same or similar safety and benefit features. This prospect is buying with emotion because the vehicle he wants will take him closer to pleasure and a false sense of confidence. A wise car salesman may ask additional questions about why the prospect feels the vehicle is a safer option. Have they looked at more economical options as the BMW is a large investment? The salesman wants the prospect to be happy with their purchase long after they drive it off the lot. They may also ask if the prospect knows anyone else who has one, or if they have ever driven a BMW 7 Series before.

In this scenario, if your prospect is on the fence about making the purchase, you can add value by helping them visualize themselves driving through their neighborhood in their new BMW and how it will make them feel. You are tying your product back to the problem it solves: filling an insecurity void, instilling confidence, and protecting their loved ones with safety features.

In the examples provided above, these situations entail discovery questions and digging into bigger problems the prospect is looking to solve. These may not happen in your initial prospecting efforts and more than likely once you are beyond the initial prospecting phase. However, understanding how your product or solution helps solve customer problems is extremely important if your goal is to accelerate and improve the results from your prospecting.

Understanding the value you bring to your prospects and the large business problems your product or service solves allows you to message effectively with intention and grab the attention of hard-to-reach decision-makers.

7

FRIEND OR FOE? KNOWING YOUR COMPETITION

Unless you work for a company that has a monopoly in their niche or market, then you have competition. Heck, even Amazon has competition. While I would argue that Amazon's continued digital transformation efforts put them in a league of their own with little to no competition, their business units can be broken down into markets and sub-niches where each has their own competitive landscape.

The start of every business plan begins with an assessment of need or desire and a market's willingness to trade currency for the product or service. One of the fastest ways to determine demand is by identifying your competition. One of the fastest ways to grow your sales and improve your prospecting is to know your competition better than they know themselves.

Coca-Cola knows Pepsi, and Pepsi knows Coca-Cola. Uber knows Lyft, and Lyft knows Uber. Google knows Apple, and Apple knows Google.

In order to understand how you position the value and competitive advantage you bring, it is imperative to understand what your competitors sell, how they pitch it, and most importantly, their strengths and weaknesses and how they are perceived by potential buyers.

Don't Be Negative

Before I touch on assessing your competitors, I must mention avoiding a critical mistake many salespeople make in their customer pursuits. I've also made this mistake a few times in the past when I was in the heat of a competitive pursuit. I'm here to tell you to *avoid* this at all costs.

Never speak negatively about your competitors in front of a prospect or customer. In fact, don't do it at all. If there is anything that makes you look weak and insecure, it's talking negatively about your competitors. It's just poor practice all around.

Top performers diligently study their competitors but never speak ill of them because they are confident and secure in their abilities. When you are confident in yourself, there is zero reason to speak negatively about other people, companies, or their offer. It accomplishes nothing other than casting you and your company in a negative light.

The Competitive Landscape

How do we position ourselves against or above our competition?

First, we must start by understanding our competitive landscape. Essentially, who are all the competitors in our industry, market, geographic region, or territory? Furthermore, who are the companies or people who sell products and services that may not be direct competitors but could find themselves in our lane to possibly seize business opportunities that we are after?

Remember, don't get stuck, do your best, and refine later.

You can quickly do some research with a couple of clicks to identify this information.

Really Know Your Competition

Now that you have established your competitive landscape, it's important to understand what your competitors bring to the market as products or services, essentially their *offer*. Moreover, you'll want to do some research to understand not only *what* they sell but also *how* they sell and market it.

If you are an employee of an organization, it is likely that this information will be provided to you at a high level by your leadership and through training. However, in my experience, it's better to do your own homework and come up with your own perspective, then marry that up with the information provided to you. In all my years of selling, I've often found that the information provided to me, while very good because I work for a great organization, was boiled down for the masses because it had to be consumable. However, I needed to know for myself to fully understand what was happening in the real world, in order to apply it correctly to help me succeed in my role.

How your competitors position themselves in the market versus how they actually show up and deliver to a customer can be very different. For example, many companies market themselves using the following taglines: Industry-Leading, Longest Running Company, #1 Ranked, Top Ranked.

While these are typical marketing terms, none of your prospects really care about them. What they do care about is how a company solves their problem and delivers as promised after signing on the dotted line. These same prospects equally don't care to hear you use a competitors' inflated marketing terms against them or to position yourself as a better brand, company, or person to buy from.

By better understanding your competitors, you can begin

to understand their strengths and weaknesses, which will allow you to craft a value-based, differentiated message. Your message will never mention your competitors or others in your industry, but it will fill the void you have identified that exists in the marketplace that solves your prospects' problems. If you have value to add, there is always an angle you can take in your approach through research, well-prepared questions, listening, and anchoring yourself to the critical outcomes your prospect is seeking.

A few ways to research your competition (there are many more, but this is a good starting point):

- Review their website (all site pages)
- Review all relevant social media platforms and posts (follow them)
- Go through their sales funnels (all the way through)
- Sign up for their email distribution list to get sales campaign emails
- Download their content (white paper, ebook, mini-training)
- Read Google reviews
- Read press releases
- Google it (You'll be surprised what you find)
- Review annual and quarterly earnings if publicly traded
- Interview your prospects or current customers
- Build relationships with former employees

Lastly: *build relationships with your competitors!*
What?
Yes, you heard me right. Let me explain...
I'm not suggesting that you need to become best friends with your competitors. However, I am saying that establishing a relationship where you can speak to your

competitors about struggles they face in a territory, account, or in the industry can be wildly beneficial. Getting to know your competitors better through relationship building has numerous other benefits. Most salespeople like to talk and relationship building comes fairly naturally to them. If you listen intently enough and ask good questions, you'll be surprised by what they tell you! You can always learn something from others if you keep an open mind. Those who are humble and constantly seek opportunities to grow and improve will win in the long run, so don't overlook your competition.

Additionally, there is usually more than enough business out there for everyone to be extremely successful.

SWOT Analysis

Now that you have identified your competitive landscape and assessed your competitors, it's good practice to document your competitors' strengths and weaknesses. You don't need to spend countless hours on this activity, but it is important to take your research and put together a quick SWOT analysis on each of your major competitors. SWOT is an acronym for Strengths, Weaknesses, Opportunities, and Threats.

While I like the traditional SWOT analysis, for this exercise, I like to shorten the acronym to SWD (Strengths, Weaknesses, Differentiators). The SWD analysis will organize your information and provide a visual reference point of your competitors and help you understand where they are strong, weak, and ultimately, how they position themselves in the marketplace. The last category, Differentiator, is the value lever that your competitors tie themselves to as it's what makes them different.

Your Value Differentiator

In a world where many salespeople are selling nearly the same product or service, your ability to quickly differentiate yourself on a sales call without mentioning your competition becomes extremely important. This becomes even more important if you are attempting to unpin an incumbent with your client that has been doing business with your prospect for any period of time.

If you're no different than them, then why should the prospect go through all the hassle of making a change? I can't tell you how many prospects I've encountered in both B2B and B2C markets that were clearly unhappy with their current situation but were unwilling to change if the offer:

- Didn't clearly display a substantial increase in value.
- Didn't offer a new opportunity or experience.
- Didn't provide a compelling enough reason to make a change.

Modern buyers are highly sophisticated when it comes to fending off salespeople and keeping you at arm's length. The primary reason, they feel that if they've heard it once, they've heard it a thousand times. Essentially, all salespeople sound the same, have the same offer, sell the same stuff, and do little in terms of differentiation.

So, that begs the following question: Why should your prospect or customer take a meeting with you when they've already met all of your competitors?

After answering the first question, the next questions you need to ask yourself are: Who cares? So what?

This is your value differentiator. In other words, it is what makes you different from your competition and the compelling reason why a prospect should take time out of their busy day to meet with you.

The reason for this ties back to the chapter on Value Creation. If your answer is focused entirely around features, benefits, or stats, you lose.

10 *Bad* Responses to "Who cares? So what!"

1. We are the biggest company in our industry. (Who cares?)
2. We are the oldest company in our industry. (So what?)
3. We are ranked #1 in our industry. (Who cares?)
4. We have proprietary (insert your B.S. proprietary whatever). (So what?)
5. We've got the best process. (Who cares?)
6. We are the first in our industry to... (Who cares?)
7. We have the lowest prices. (So what?)
8. We have superior quality. (So what?)
9. Our technology is industry-leading and better than our competitors. (Who cares?)
10. We have the brightest minds in the industry developing and enhancing our products. (So what?)

Now you may be scratching your head thinking, *All major companies use these taglines, features, and benefits to market and sell their product.* You are correct; they do market these features and benefits to further convince a prospect to buy. However, that's not what the most successful companies are selling. They are selling the outcome. The features, benefits, stats, and brand recognition are icing on the cake. After all, doesn't it seem that everyone claims to be the best at what they sell? That tagline lost its luster in our prospects' eyes long ago.

As I've mentioned several times throughout this book,

people buy products and services to help them achieve their desired outcomes. They don't buy for bells and whistles, unless it brings them closer to their desired outcome.

To help cement this thought in your head further, look no further than Apple and Steve Jobs, one of the most influential inventors, creators, and marketers of our time.

Jobs had many successful sales and marketing strategies we all can learn from, but two of them are extremely applicable here.

In "10 Steve Jobs Marketing Lessons and His Famous Marketing Quotes," Camila Villafane, blogger at Postcron, wrote the following:

STEVE JOBS MARKETING LESSON #2: DON'T SELL PRODUCTS, SELL DREAMS.

Apple's strategy involves selling their consumers a global package of dreams, personal experiences, and status, and it makes almost all other products go unnoticed if they don't carry the Apple logo...

STEVE JOBS MARKETING LESSON #3: FOCUS ON THE EXPERIENCE

Think different. Think like Nike and Apple.

Focus on creating a universe of sensations, experiences, and values that the person gets when they buy your product. Analyze how it feels to use and buy your products, and think about what you need to improve, and what you need to focus on.[1]

If one of the greatest inventors and marketers in our lifetime focused on experiences and dreams, which are outcomes rather than product features, then it would be wise for the rest of us to follow suit as we look to rapidly grow our sales and earn more income.

Lastly, as I use Jobs and Apple as an example, I want to point out that nearly every product Apple created during the iPhone, Tablet, and iPod boom already existed in the marketplace; however, Jobs packaged and marketed the products as if they never existed before. If you are reading this book, then you are selling something, and you likely have competitors selling nearly the same product or service as you are in slightly different ways. Don't let that be an excuse for why you aren't achieving your goals.

8

STOP BEING ANTI-SOCIAL

Social selling has changed the world when it comes to how buyers and sellers interact and connect. However, it hasn't changed it completely and hasn't replaced the phone, email, and face-to-face conversations. In my opinion, one of the biggest mistakes sellers can make when interacting with modern buyers is to replace traditional methods of prospecting completely with social selling. You must have both in today's world.

If you're in sales and spend any time on social media channels at all, which I hope you do, I'm sure you've seen a plethora of automation techniques and ways to automate the way that you are interacting with buyers through AI and machine learning. But there are some major flaws in that method. If you're leveraging social selling, which I must add you should be, then there are a few important topics we need to cover.

Social Selling

First, your prospects on social channels are no different than the humans you call, email, text, and meet face-to-face. They have the same wants, needs, desires, and pet peeves as the persona they represent on social media, regardless of the channel.

No matter who you're interacting with, at the end of the day, what you need to realize is they're human beings. Don't treat people on social media the way they are presented on social media: just a persona, a picture, a bio. You will fail. They are much more than that. They are a person who has goals, interests, challenges, and problems they're looking to solve in their business on a day-to-day basis. You need to approach them as such.

Prospects want to build meaningful relationships with sellers regardless of whether they're on social media channels or over the phone, text message, or in person. Even more so with social selling, modern-day buyers are extremely reluctant to interact and engage with salespeople. In fact, if your title is salesperson, account executive, or account manager, they know the reason you're reaching out to them is to sell them more stuff. So it becomes extremely difficult to engage with these modern buyers and prospects when they already have their guard up and are unwilling to engage and connect with you.

I've seen so many salespeople approach prospects through different social channels, and they treat them like meat instead of treating them like the humans they are. If you can't show up genuinely on social media, you have already lost. Just like phone, email, text message, and networking events, modern buyers and prospects can read and smell right through your sales-y behavior. They know and can tell that there's blood in the water, and you are trying to sell them something. You need to move away from that. You don't need to be afraid of trying to sell someone something as long as it helps them solve a problem. But how you show up is completely different.

You typically have one strike when it comes to interacting

with people on social media. Now, don't get me wrong, I'm not saying that you need to give up after you've attempted to reach out to a prospect on LinkedIn. But what I am saying is that if you strike out the first time by showing up inappropriately, the chance that that prospect will ever respond to you again drops drastically. While prospects are inundated with calls, emails, text messages, and LinkedIn requests on a daily basis, they still don't forget. In fact, they don't forget the really bad connections and the really bad messages they receive. This becomes increasingly important when attempting to connect with hard-to-reach executives.

Effective Social Platform Prospecting

I'm now going to touch on what I feel is the appropriate way to prospect on social platforms. You see, it doesn't need to be overly complicated. In fact, it's the same approach you would use over the phone or email and some of the more traditional prospecting methods. Just like in those methods, you build the list of prospects you're going to reach out to. Instead of sending them an email and placing a phone call, you're going to send them a connection request, regardless of the channel you're on. If it's LinkedIn, you can send them a connection request. And then you wait.

Do not pounce right away and try to start selling them something or ask them if they'd have an interest in working with you to solve business problems. They don't even know who you are yet. In fact, they haven't heard your voice and don't know your signature on your email. They likely haven't even done any research on your company.

Give it a day after connecting with them. Add them to your list, and then the next day, follow up with them and thank them for connecting with you. Be genuine about it. Personalize that same message and say something intriguing about their profile. Perhaps they wrote an article. Perhaps they commented on a post by someone else that you read. Maybe they wrote a book. Maybe they have a very high degree that they've recently earned. Personalize your message, tell them how interesting it is, and add some personal flair to it in terms of why you think it's interesting.

Add some value to the conversation. Provide them with a link to a website or an article that they might find interesting. Invite them to a networking event. Maybe strike up a conversation around how you are connected with some of the same people and you'd love to connect with them at some point.

The next time you reach out to them based on the dialogue you engage with them in, you want to start building a relationship. The way you build a relationship is you give, you don't receive. You need to constantly be giving and not taking. You need to be providing that person with value, making them feel good, and helping them understand how you can help them through valuable content, information, and intriguing questions.

Another tactic that works well is to follow all of your key prospects on social media. It seems obvious, but it is rare that sellers take action on this, even when it makes complete sense. When they post or comment on a post, comment on their post and share something of value. It could be an intriguing thought that further adds value to their post, a nice "like," an alternative point of view, or even a share to your audience while adding your own thoughts. Do enough of this, and you'll start becoming omnipresent. Whatever you do, add value just like everything else. Don't be a lurker that likes everything your prospects posts but never adds your own thoughts or ideas.

Your prospects can't blame you for following and commenting on their content because they posted on a social platform in the first place. Give it a try. You'll be surprised how it makes the aforementioned social selling steps even easier to begin generating productive dialogue with your prospects.

The final step in social selling: move the conversation offline as soon as possible. What do I mean by that? Take the conversation to the phone as soon as you can. Better yet, take the conversation to in-person. If they can't meet in-person, do a Zoom or WebEx call. You want to get face-to-face with that prospect as soon as possible to further the relationship-building process, to start getting into discovery, and to understand if there is actually a problem they're looking to solve that may align with your product or service.

Creating a Personal Brand

Lastly, I'd be wrong to not mention the importance of building a personal brand on social platforms relative to your industry. As I've mentioned before, an informed and educated seller is a powerful seller. Creating a personal brand is often overlooked by professional sellers and left to the content creators and influencers; however, that's a huge mistake. Here's why. Since we've covered how modern buyers are more sophisticated and no longer wish to buy from salespeople, instead of choosing to work with advisors and consultants, building a personal brand becomes increasingly important. So much so that if you aren't building your brand, there is a large chance that someone else you are competing against is and has a leg up on you given that they are providing valuable insight and information to the marketplace.

Leave the company marketing up to your corporation if you are a contributing sales rep, but building your brand as an expert advisor in your niche creates a massive opportunity to engage in dialogue with your prospects. Like anything else, don't expect your first or even fifteenth post of valuable content to go viral. But over time, you'll start to build momentum and create a following. There are few opportunities to change how your prospects view you, but creating a personal brand as a trusted advisor in your industry is one, if not the best, opportunity.

The good news is that you don't need to be incredibly creative or an expert copywriter. Research content that is extremely valuable in your industry, digest it, share it, AND provide your OWN thoughts and insights. A great way to identify what is getting attention is to identify other thought leaders in your niche and mirror, *not copy*, what they are doing. If they share something of value, feel free to share it with your audience, but you must add your own thoughts, insights, and opinions on the content for it to be valuable and prove that you have an opinion and expertise. Whatever you do, don't click the "Share" button without adding your own thoughts or ideas. There is no value in that.

There is another huge plus to this strategy. Through your research of valuable information to share, you're improving your business acumen and further building your wealth of knowledge in your niche. Do it enough times, and you'll become an expert in your industry, making it so much easier to open more doors to hard to reach decision-makers.

In the end, social selling is not much different than the way we sell in more traditional methods. Unfortunately, due to automation and the way that our brains are wired, we treat prospects differently on all social channels. If you want to succeed in social selling, you must humanize outreach, consistently look to add value, and begin building relationships through communication.

The next chapter focuses on one of the most important variables in sales prospecting. This concept is not revolutionary, but it's often missed or not executed properly as part of most sales prospecting efforts.

9

MULTIPLE COMMUNICATION MEDIUM FRAMEWORK (MCMF)

While prior chapters are critical to your success, the perfect blueprint for B2B selling includes leveraging all communication mediums available to you in order to reach your prospects.

Up to this point, I've covered the importance of being omnipresent and showing up wherever your customers spend their time. Unfortunately, for a variety of reasons, which I'll touch on briefly, sellers often get stuck behind one communication medium. While tactical in practice, the strategy by which you perform customer outreach is massively important to your success.

Your Communication Channel

Given the growth of the digital world, I continue to witness hungry sellers in both B2B and B2C markets rely on only one of several communication mediums available to them in order to set more appointments, continue a sales pursuit, and close more deals.

Look at your own prospecting efforts and be really honest with yourself. How many of the following communication channels do you use and what percentage do you use each channel?

- Office phone calls
- Mobile phone calls
- Text messaging
- Email
- Unpaid social media outreach direct messaging
- Direct mail (snail mail)
- Paid traffic (social media advertising)
- Email marketing
- Chatbots
- Networking events/Industry events

For most, the answer will likely be 80-90% two communication channels: email and phone. This leaves a lot of untapped opportunities on the table.

Your prospects aren't always on email. They are also not always by their desk phone. They may never answer phone calls from unknown numbers on their cell phone. They may have their cell phones turned off or on silent for the majority of the day.

With that said, it's highly likely that they are plugged in to one of these communication mediums several times a day at very specific times.

For example, if you primarily rely on emailing prospects throughout the day, never placing a phone call, what if the prospect isn't the type to respond to external emails? What if they receive hundreds of emails per day and yours gets buried after one hour? What if all external emails hit their spam folder?

I know I get very behind on emails throughout the day, only paying attention to emails that are of high priority involving prospects, customers, and leadership. Everything else falls to the bottom of my inbox.

If you're an email-only sales rep, and you're not getting much love back from prospects in the form of replies, you're likely feeling stuck. How can you expect to succeed?

You don't have to be stuck. Over the years, the best way I've been able to cement the idea of MCMF into reps I mentor is by asking them to step in their customer's shoes.

Close your eyes for a minute. I'd like you to pretend you are now the prospect. A salesperson is trying to contact you to set an appointment to discuss their offer, which could potentially help you solve a problem. Now, I'd like you to answer the following questions:

- What would be the best way to get in touch with you: phone, email, text, or social media?
- What would be the best time to contact you by phone?
- How often do you respond to emails and texts from people you don't know?

The answers for you will likely be different than mine. What we do know is that in today's busy world, buyers are busier than ever and are inundated with emails and calls from salespeople on a daily basis.

If you only tried to reach me via email, I'd likely click delete each time until I permanently set up a filter to send your emails directly to my spam folder.

On the other hand, you may be the cold caller only type. So, what's wrong with this? The fact that you are picking up the phone is fantastic. You are already winning. Most reps avoid the phone at all costs due to fear and lack of skill. But you are still leaving meat on the bone.

What percentage of your prospects pick up the phone? Maybe it's a pretty high percentage.

Are you calling only landline numbers given to you by whatever lead generation tool you're using?

You may be asking yourself, "Which mediums of communication are best?" or "Which ones should I use?"

The answer is all of them, but not all at once.

If your goal is to become omnipresent, your name needs to roll off your prospect's tongue when they think of a business problem that your product or service solves.

To achieve this, you need to develop a proper sales cadence. A sales cadence strategy is a critical step in your overall sales prospecting strategy. In the next chapter, I will discuss the various parts of what I believe to be most important in a sales cadence, along with a guide to follow based on your industry.

Valuable Insights Action Step

Are you ready to continue to utilize The Intelligence Factor with your prospecting? Go to your *Ready. Aim. Fire Workbook* and complete the exercises and questions for Part II. Within the workbook, identify your prospect's problem and desired future state and recognize your product's value.

To access your complimentary *Ready. Aim. Fire Workbook*, go to www.TheIntelligenceFactor.com/freeworkbook

PART III

BUILDING MOMENTUM

10

DON'T. GET. STUCK.

I n 2008, we were in the middle of the largest economic downturn since the Great Recession. I sat in my open cubicle amongst many other hungry salespeople, watching tenured account executives down to the most junior sales reps struggle to make sales. Customers weren't buying. After coming out of the mortgage industry where the downturn started, the faces on the sales reps were all too familiar to me. They were unsure when to call their customers, how to approach them, and which mediums to use. They were mostly staring at their computer screens or surfing social media, waiting for the phone to ring. There were a few exceptions. There were four or five very talented reps who were still earning large six-figure incomes.

There was one senior rep who had an office in my direct line of sight from my desk. He was an absolute killer. I'd watch him day in and day out as his sales results continued to climb, yet the majority of the office was complaining about lack of business and prospects unwilling to take meetings with them since they had no money to spend on projects. I was still new to the organization, and while I came in with a fire lit inside of me, I was a too timid to talk to one of the more senior sellers at the time. Once I mustered up the courage to chat with the guy, I asked him what his secret to success was while most everyone else was floundering in the tough economic conditions. He gave me a piece of advice that has stuck with me the past twelve years.

> *"Most salespeople aren't selling anything because they aren't reaching out to their customers through all the avenues available to them. Use them all. Be everywhere!"*

I've never forgotten those words of advice. It's simple and makes sense, like most things in life that work. Usually, we get in our own way.

Frozen by Uncertainty

Most salespeople get "stuck" in not knowing how, when, what, and how often to reach out to prospects to grab their attention.

The salesperson reaches out via phone to the prospect at a random time throughout the day with little research done on the company or person and leaves a voicemail that is all about their company and product or service and little about the prospect and their business.

They send an email with their fingers crossed that the prospect responds back some time that week, although they know the odds are stacked against them.

The salesperson then leaves a second voicemail and sends a second email the following week. *The end.* They feel stuck, so they move on.

I've been there before, wondering:

- What's the best way to reach out to a prospect for the first time?

- What communication medium do I use the
  second time if I didn't get a response?
- How long do I wait between attempted contacts?
- How many times do I call the prospect?
- How many emails vs. phone calls?
- Is a text message acceptable?
- Do I leave a voicemail every time?
- When do I give up?

These questions only scratch the surface of *what's* on the minds of sales reps. While sales prospecting is definitely an art form and requires a level of intuition, when performed correctly, a sales cadence can double and even triple your results.

In the last chapter, I highlighted the importance of leveraging the Multiple Communication Medium Framework or MCMF. Leveraging all communication mediums available to you along with a valuable compelling message can make the difference between exceeding your sales quotas and not hitting them at all.

Furthermore, having a proper sales cadence methodology allows a salesperson to follow a well laid-out plan that allows them to move into execution mode instead of getting stuck wondering what their next move should be.

Make Contact

In my years selling and leading salespeople, by far the number one issue I find is that sales reps greatly lack the required attempted contacts to the prospects they want to work with.

Gabe Larsen, VP of Marketing at Kustomer, wrote *The Definitive Guide to Sales Cadence.*[1] Larsen's work shares insights based on his previous work at XANT as their VP of Growth. The data he shares is based on hundreds of thousands of inbound and outbound cadences and over 1.5 million activities that Larsen and his XANT Lab team studied. I highly recommend reading the full report for additional data-driven research on sales cadences. In his book, Larsen shared:

> We performed a survey and asked over 1000 companies how many touches they executed on a lead or contact and the total number was 15.4. That 15. 4 breaks down to 4.7 calls, 4.6 emails, 2.9 voicemails, 1.8 social touches, 0.8 mailers, 0.7 text messages. But that's what they 'said' they did.

When XANT examined what reps actually did, they found that "the typical inbound cadence has 4.05 attempts and the typical outbound cadence has 3 attempts."

This is data-backed proof that what sales reps "say" they do versus what they actually do is very different. Clearly, three attempts per contact or lead is not nearly enough to see the results salespeople are after, yet it happens again and again for new and tenured sales professionals.

Why is there such a disconnect? I have my theories based on experience. These include fear, uncertainty of the proper cadence, lack of practice, lack of expertise in their niche, and confusion on the type of content and message to deliver to their prospects.

What is the appropriate amount of touches a salesperson should make to be most effective? You've likely heard anything from *Just keep smiling and dialing* to make *10-15 attempted contacts per lead or contact.*

According to XANT's data, the cadences that yield the best results are as follows:

Inbound Lead-Based (rep reaching out to someone who knows your company via white paper, free trial, demo, web form completion)

- Phone, VM, Email, Social, Direct Mail, Text = Up
  to 10 total touches

<u>Outbound</u> (Rep reaching out to a prospect that doesn't know your company via email, phone or other communication mediums).

- Phone, Voicemail, Email, Social, Direct Mail, Text
  = Up to 8 total touches

While the suggested touches provide a sweet spot target, it doesn't necessarily mean that doing more yields negative results, it just doesn't prove that your results will be better.

Split Testing

I love making business decisions using data. It is the most trusted source of information we have at our disposal. You need to find what works best for you. How? You need to engage in enough activity and track your results.

John Barrows, expert sales trainer, author, and owner of J. Barrows Sales Training, has often recommended a strategy when it comes to prospecting and other parts of your sales cycle that I've been implementing for years. I honestly didn't have a name for it, it was something I just did to get my own data to find what was working. After several years of learning how marketers think and attack the market, I found that this is something they also use to identify winning ad campaigns.

So what is it? Split testing.

The purpose of split testing, or A/B testing, is to take two variables, in this case, two different sales cadences, messages, or approaches, execute each of them, and log your results. You then compare the data from approach A to approach B to identify which approach worked best.

You can scale your split tests as much as you desire, but in my experience, it's better to test two cadences for a designated period of time and then choose the cadence that produced the best results. If you desire, you can consistently run split tests on your sales cadences to continue to refine. This is a good approach over time if you collect the data properly, as customers evolve along with technology and economic conditions.

Before you can split test your sales cadence, you need to determine the structure or components. Generally, there are five components that make up a sales cadence:

1. Timing: The time of day you reach out to a prospect or lead
2. Frequency: The time or space between attempted contacts
3. Attempts: The number of attempted contacts you make to reach a prospect
4. Messaging: The content used in your message
5. Medium: The communication medium used (Phone, VM, Email, Social, Text, Direct Mail)

In the next few chapters, you will learn more about these components and how to use them to make powerful changes with your sales cadence and prospecting sales.

11

TIMING, FREQUENCY, AND ATTEMPTS

I f you've ever felt like you were calling prospects for hours on end with little results to show for your effort, you're not alone. I've been there many times. It even happens to the most talented salespeople, but they have the skills to quickly dial in their timing. *When* you call prospects can be critically important in your ability to contact hard-to-reach buyers and, if done correctly, can be a definite game-changer.

Timing isn't exclusive to phone calls either. The timing aspect of your sales cadence should include phone, voicemail, email, text, and social media. Direct mail isn't really as important here other than the time of year you send direct mail to ensure your prospect receives your content. If you know they will be on vacation during the holidays, send your mail ahead of time.

Top Days

When considering timing, think about the best times of the day and the best days of the week to improve your odds of reaching your customers.

Larsen's data shows that the best days to call are Wednesday and Thursday, compared to the worst day, Tuesday. Based on this data, the success rate of reaching a customer by phone is nearly 50% higher on Thursday than Tuesday. You may be wondering why there is such a stark difference in contact rates. The reason is fairly simple: most businesses today don't take a break over the weekend and issues pile up. Decision-makers typically spend Monday and Tuesday getting caught up from the weekend, digging themselves out of a hole. By Wednesday and Thursday, they are finally coming up for air and getting into their weekly rhythm.

Prime Times

If Wednesday and Thursday are the best days to call, when are the best times to call?

According to Larsen, data suggests between 8-9 AM and 6-7 PM throughout the week, with the exception of Friday afternoons being a bad time to call as prospects are shutting down for the weekend.

While the above data does produce a compelling argument and gives you a baseline weekday and hourly plan to follow, it doesn't mean that the data is 100% accurate.

In 2011, I was attempting to break into a large Fortune 200 company for the first time. It had been years since our organization had done any substantial business with the particular business unit I was focused on. I spent months calling and emailing at different times of the day and week. Slowly but surely, I better understood the company's business cycle and weekly business activities through contacts I had made with decision-makers and non-decision-makers. What I found was that each sub-department within the business operated differently. Some decision-makers did fit Larsen's data to be most reachable on Wednesdays and

Thursdays. For others, Monday and Friday during the lunch hour were best.

I found that the time of day to yield the highest contact rates were:

- 7-9 AM (Don't worry about bugging your prospect. If they are anyone worth selling to, they've been up for hours)
- 11-1:30 PM (Catching your prospects during their lunch hour is perfectly acceptable and a great time to make contact with them. They are likely in a better mood as they are taking a break from the madness)
- 4-6:30 PM (Your customers are winding down their day and likely at their desk, by their phone, and catching up on emails for the day)

Remember, all prospects now have a smartphone near them 100% of the time, so get their digits!

Making This Happen

While these time blocks aren't the latest and greatest cold calling invention, they work incredibly well. Unfortunately, most reps completely sabotage their results due to laziness and lack of discipline. This may require you to get up an hour earlier, skip lunch with your colleagues, and skip the after-work happy hour. If you want it badly enough, you have to make some sacrifices. To me, these are incredibly small sacrifices to make for the results they deliver, but only you can decide if you're willing to make these changes in your behaviors and decisions.

Most companies have morning meetings that may range anywhere between 7:30-9 AM to get their teams organized, set plans for the day, and establish goals and commitments.

There is a fundamental problem with this in that this is during one of the most important times to prospect. If you aren't in charge of your own schedule and are being mandated to attend each morning meeting by your leadership, I suggest sitting down with them to ask your leader what the main goal is for the organization. The answer should be to grow sales and create more opportunities. If that's the goal, why would you pull your starting lineup during some of the most important times of the game? Have the conversation. Make a commitment to be ultra prepared and spend your time in the mornings reaching out to customers to engage in dialogue. When you start seeing results, there should be little argument from your sales leaders.

How you start your day determines how the rest of it will go. Start off strong by focusing on what's most important.

Timing Framework

What I have found is that the fastest way to understand what works for each client is the two-pronged framework below. This approach will rapidly increase your contact rate if you execute with urgency and curiosity. In many cases, you just need to ask the most simple questions.

Split Test Timing

Run this split test for a minimum of 30 days before changing to allow time to acquire data; *more on this later in the frequency section.*
Daily:

- Split Test 1
- Wednesday: Call & VM
- Thursday: Call & email

- Friday: Social media
- <u>Split Test 2</u>
- Monday: Call & VM
- Wednesday: Social media
- Friday: Call & email

Hourly:

- <u>Split Test 1</u>
- Wednesday: Call between 7-9 AM & leave voicemail
- Thursday: Call between 4-6:30 PM & send email
- Friday: 7:30am Social media connection w/ message
- <u>Split Test 2</u>
- Monday: Call between 11-1 PM & leave voicemail
- Wednesday: 7:30 AM Social media connection w/ message
- Friday: Call between 7-9 AM & send email

The reason for the early social touches is that most people check their social media messages when they wake up and when they arrive to work. Typically, they will see the message and can reply from their phone app to connect, and if you're lucky, a reply to your personalized message. As a reminder, your message will not include setting up a meeting with the person in your first social outreach.

Once you've tested these days and times for 30 days, assess your results. If you are making progress with one or two particular days and times, *great*, but your job isn't over. You want to continually test your timing cadence. This requires some tracking in your CRM or in an Excel database, but once you have it built, you just input your data after each call block.

When setting up your next split test, take your winning

cadence, and test it against a new cadence of different days and times. It's best to continue testing as time goes on until you've become so ingrained in your prospect's organization that they are now a customer and you are on a texting basis, or you have built so solid a foundation with your prospects that you can text them and get a response at anytime.

Still, even to this day, I find myself testing different timing cadences with current customers as their responsibilities and schedules are ever-changing, which keeps me on my toes, never getting too comfortable.

Bottom Up

While I'm a huge proponent of a top-down approach for many reasons, don't dismiss the little people. Okay, they aren't actually small, and I don't mean to be condescending. The non-decision makers inside your future customers are incredibly valuable to our prospect's businesses, but why is it that salespeople overlook these people inside their target customers?

These contacts include the secretary, the line worker at an assembly plant, the waitress at a restaurant, a manager, a salesperson, a software engineer, and many other titles that people hold within an organization that are not decision-maker level. While not complicated whatsoever, this may be the easiest way to determine the appropriate timing cadence for each of your target customers. This is incredibly simple, but again, often missed by sellers.

Whether you are the owner of your own business or a contributing salesperson, I'd like you to reverse engineer your thinking. If a sales rep was trying to get a hold of your boss or you for that matter, who else would be a good person for them to call that may know your schedule or your boss's schedule? For me, I have direct reports, peers, and leaders who all have a pretty good idea when I'd be most available to take a call or respond to an email. After all, they can just look at my calendar and share my schedule. If you were trying to contact my boss, I'd tell you to call him between 7-7:45 AM, 11:30-1 PM, and 4:30-5:30 PM, and the best days to reach him would be Wednesday, Thursday, and Friday. I may even give you his email and cell phone number if you treat me right and show me that you value my role and responsibilities in the company.

Hopefully, the point I'm making is ringing loud and clear to you. Identify targets inside your target customers who are non-buyers that may have the information you're after. If you're selling to small and medium-sized businesses, you may need to get a little creative if you can't find these people via your typical lead generation channel or social media. Regardless, seek them out and treat them like gold. Salespeople rarely treat them like they are worth their time. Take them out for coffee or lunch. They will be ecstatic to spend a little time with you.

In the process of forging a relationship, ask them the simple question: "If I needed to get a hold of _____, what is the best day and time to do so? And what is the most effective way to reach them?"

If you are able to start building a relationship with them, ask for an introduction. Don't make your life harder than it needs to be.

Text Timing

In regards to email and text timing, you can email and text any day of the week; however, it will be important that you time them correctly as part of your overall sales cadence. There are a few rules to follow in regards to email and text to improve your odds and not irritate prospects.

These are general guidelines. If things are working for

you, don't be afraid to mix things up and get a little aggressive from time to time.

There have certainly been times when I've gone outside of these guidelines and seen success. I just recommend working within these guidelines for email and text 90% of the time.

Email:

- Send emails five minutes before or five minutes after the hour to ensure they hit the top of your prospect's inbox when they are checking emails on their mobile device after a meeting has concluded.
- Don't email prospects consecutively every day of the week.
- Time your emails in correspondence to your phone, VM, and text cadence.

Text:

- I don't recommend texting a prospect out of the blue before 7 AM or after 7 PM if you've never made contact with them. (If you have a legitimate relationship or connection with the company or someone this person knows, this may not apply.)
- Texting can be a gamble depending on the person and organization. You'll have to test it at times and use non-decision makers who may know the prospect to understand if that type of communication is welcome or not. In some cases, you'll just need to give it a shot.

Frequency and Attempts

For sales prospecting, frequency can be defined as the duration of time between each event or attempted contact. Attempts refer to the number of attempted touches per contact or prospect. While they mean different things, there is congruence in their meaning.

Frequency and attempted touchpoints are something of a confusing point for many sellers. Too many touchpoints too close together, and you run the risk of irritating your prospect. Too little and too far apart, and you'll never accomplish your goal of making contact with the target customer. A decade ago, I wouldn't have included social media touches in this equation of reaching out to a prospect with too much frequency, but given the continual rise of digitally and socially driven behavior, it must be included.

When it comes to the frequency and attempted contact number that guarantees your ability to reach a prospect, there is plenty of advice and evidence that suggests that as the continual outreaches increase, your contact rate will also increase. As I covered earlier, Larsen's data along with a broad spectrum of other statistical analyses prove that the magic number is eight attempted contacts or touchpoints.

Based on my experience, I would agree that by eight attempts via MCMF, I'll have reached my prospect via one of those mediums. There is one caveat to this data that is critical to long-term success. While the statistics may prove that beyond eight attempts, you start experiencing the law of diminishing returns, I'd argue that giving up completely is also wrong. Giving up is never the answer, at least not in the long run.

Just last year, I finally made contact with a C-Level executive I had been attempting to contact for over a year. I applied MCMF and split tested a multitude of different cadences, striking out week after week. After one year of continual testing and not giving up, I finally made contact with him via text message. That year of work turned into huge profits over a three month period for my company, but in the long term, the relationship has led to seven-figure recurring revenue and growth in our partnership.

During my pursuit of this particular executive, what I didn't do was give up after eight attempts. What I did was apply short breaks in between each series of eight attempts. During those breaks, I used other resources in and outside the company to gain intel and establish a relationship with someone who trusted me enough to share his cell phone number. Wouldn't you know it, I texted the executive at 7:30 AM on a Friday, leveraging the insightful information I had collected, which I knew would be valuable to him if he met with me. Why didn't my previous attempts work? More on that later.

Based on my tested methods compared to research from a variety of trusted sources, the frequency cadence that has worked the best for me is as follows:

Day 1: Outreach
Day 1: Secondary Outreach
Day 5: Outreach
Day 10: Outreach
Day 10: Secondary Outreach
Day 15: Outreach
Day 15: Secondary Outreach
Day 20: Outreach
Day 25: Outreach
Day 25: Secondary Outreach
Day 30: Outreach
Day 30: Email Outreach (Break if needed)

Typically, I reach the prospect between Day 5 and Day 10, but there are certainly times when I have to court the prospect through a series of communications over a 30 day period.

As I've provided you with a frequency framework to follow over the course of a monthly period, you may be wondering what to do next if you don't make contact with your prospect. This has happened to me many times over the years, and it will continue to happen with certain targets as each human being and company is different.

As mentioned in my prior story about the executive I recently engaged with, I struck out time and time again and took multiple breaks during my pursuit of achieving a meeting with him.

What you do during these breaks is just as important as what you do while prospecting the target. When you take a break from attempting to contact a target prospect, I suggest the following:

Review all of your email communications over the past 30 days (if you really want to make data-driven decisions, track all of your communication: voicemail, email, text, social, etc.).

Call any relevant relationships you have made inside the organization:

- Share the messaging you have used.
- Ask for feedback as to why they think they aren't responding.
- Work with them to identify hot buttons you can use in your messaging to grab the prospect's attention.

Do more research on the following information to be used in your messaging:

- Strategic priorities for the company
- Trends and industry challenges
- Major competitor landscape changes
- Identify incumbent partnerships

The timing of your sales cadence is extremely important in increasing your success rate in contacting your target buyers. So, consider the above frameworks and methods and give them a try. Test and retest different methods but use the frameworks as a guide on how to build what works for your industry, your offer, and your prospects.

While the frequency used above may be what has worked best for me and what data suggests, your industry and customer may require a different frequency. Whatever you do, don't get stuck after four attempts because you aren't sure what to do next.

12

MESSAGING

O ver the last twelve years, I've tested a multitude of different frequency cadences along with a tracked number of attempts. However, the number one factor that led me to make contact with the prospect and set up an appointment was not the frequency or cadence at all; it was the content or message I delivered being something relevant to their business.

Quality + Quantity = SUCCESS

Over time, my studies of marketing and advertising have greatly helped me understand how much salespeople can learn from email marketing. While I don't personally use broad sweeping email marketing campaigns in B2B sales, especially strategic selling, what you can learn from storytelling and sequencing of information through a frequency of touches, can be instrumental in your success.

While sequence and frequency do matter, what is just as, if not more, important, is the message you deliver in your communication outreach. Send the wrong message 12 times during a 30 day period, and you'll turn your customers off.

Your phone calls will continue to be ignored, your voicemails deleted, and your emails flagged to be sent straight to the SPAM folder.

Send valuable, insightful messages through storytelling, and you'll be looked at as an advisor to your prospects before they've even met with you.

When I started out selling in the B2B marketplace in 2008, I approached my prospecting with a vengeance. I had come from several successful years in the mortgage sales industry, which required a high quantity of calls coupled with plenty of emails to prospects. When I moved to B2B sales in the recession, I was hungry as I saw the opportunity in front of me regardless of the economic conditions. At the time, I knew very little about call blocks and the potential value of breaking up my day into bite-sized chunks. Instead, I figuratively glued the phone to my ear and never put it down. I had two goals at the time:

1. Make more calls than everyone on my team as I saw them as internal competition
2. Make more calls than all of my competitors

In my opinion, all successful sellers are extremely competitive and use their *why* to drive their actions and activities on a daily basis. Sales does come down to a law of averages, regardless of your approach in most cases. More outreach should equal more opportunities to make contact with the prospect and engage in a valuable conversation. It certainly does to an extent. You can't expect to succeed in sales with low amounts of quantity. However, you also won't succeed focusing entirely on quantity while severely lacking in the quality department.

Unfortunately, many sales leaders preach and hound their sales teams to focus on more and more quantity while quality goes out the window.

So it begs the question: is it our sales leaders' faults or the reps themselves? In my opinion, both parties are at fault.

The sales leaders are attempting to drive the right level of necessary activity. Unfortunately, too often, they don't show and teach the salesperson how to spend the appropriate amount of time conducting prospect research while holding themselves accountable to a measurable level of outreach inputs.

Sales reps often hide their fear of picking up the phone with "more customer research." Alternatively, they call everyone on their list with no plan, no value message, and land a few meetings but never make it long term. They don't increase their level of expertise or deliver a value-focused message that is directly tied to the target prospect's problems.

For the record, I'll always take the latter salesperson over the first as long as they are willing to learn and educate themselves. Imperfect action will always trump perfect inaction.

Personalized Messaging

From 2008-2010, texting was certainly possible but not used often, and social selling really had not yet come alive. Therefore, I relied heavily on phone, voicemail, email, and even direct mail for executive-level decision-makers. For the first few years, I was able to massively scale my business, break new accounts, and crush my goals from my effort alone.

As the years passed, I was given larger enterprise accounts to break into. These companies were more complex and had many barriers to entry. Starting over from scratch can be a daunting task for anyone, but after some time, I had built up enough confidence and skill that I knew I'd be able to crack any target customer with enough focused effort.

It was at this time that I started noticing that the phone

wasn't working as well as it had in the past. I was calling prospects using a well-tested sales cadence but not having much luck. Prospects were using cell phones more often for voice and email. Email was becoming incredibly important. The majority of my prospects were in meetings all day and rarely available by desk phone. If they were at their desk, they weren't taking my calls nor were they returning them.

At the time, I was working very closely with a regional sales leader who has become a friend and trusted mentor I'd still call to this day for advice.

Bi-weekly, we'd review my progress in each of the accounts we shared in our portfolio. In our review sessions, we'd review the prospects within the accounts where I wasn't gaining any traction. Let me be the first to tell you, in my top target account, I wasn't getting anywhere! As we took a deeper dive into my messaging, we identified several issues:

My elevator speech, voicemails, and emails were too long, all about me and my company, didn't provide any value or insight that I knew about my prospects' business challenges, and didn't explain how we help other similar customers.

As a side note, I'm not a fan of scripted elevator speeches. I've never met someone that loved their elevator speech. Nearly all elevator speeches sound cheesy and inauthentic. This is the primary reason that I don't provide scripted elevator speeches in this book.

In our review of my messaging, it was clear that I wasn't grabbing the prospect's attention and creating interest because my approach was too generalized.

Using the same message with a varied audience was no longer working.

Many sales professionals start their careers out very young, just as I did. When you are in your early twenties, calling on prospects who are at least twice your age and with twice the experience can be a daunting task mentally and physically. What's worse is that prospects know that many salespeople are young. They know that with youth comes inexperience.

Unfortunately, this comes with some potentially negative consequences. When you are early in your sales career, your inexperience combined with hustle may earn you opportunities due to the sheer amount of effort you put into your prospecting, but your future customers may not treat you with the respect you desire.

AIDA

In order to overcome this challenge, your sales messaging must be crafted in a well-articulated, concise manner that grabs your prospect's attention. Your sales message can and will vary based on whether or not your prospect is in your Tier 1, Tier 2 or Tier 3 account categories, but overall, you should strive to produce a short, compelling message that:

- Grabs the prospect's attention
- Generates interest
- Creates credibility
- Helps them make a decision
- Shows them how to take action

This is also known by the acronym AIDA, which was developed in 1898 by advertising pioneer E. St. Elmo Lewis.[1] It adds credibility to the equation as attention and interest are helped along by credibility.

AIDA is essentially the steps that a prospect or prospective customer goes through before they make the decision to buy a product or service.

A: You must get the prospect's *attention*.

I: You must get them *interested*.

D: They must have *desire*.

A: You must help them take *action*.

In your prospecting efforts, this is the top challenge most sellers must overcome. In order to do this, I recommend thinking about what it is you and your company do for your customers.

As you think about this, as I mentioned in a prior chapter, refrain from using words and phrases like:

- We
- I
- My company
- I work for
- We are the largest...
- Leading company...
- Industry-leading...

Again, those phrases and words are on the "no-no" list as they are all about you, not about your prospect.

In order to generate interest and grab the prospect's attention, you must focus on three things:

- What business problem is your prospect and/or their industry trying to solve?
- How does your company help?
- Who have you helped?

To put some context around this strategy, let's look at a few examples of email, phone, and voicemail value messaging that are attention-grabbing, generate interest, and build credibility.

As mentioned in an earlier chapter, when delivering a message, regardless of the communication medium, put yourself in your prospect's shoes and ask yourself *What's In It For Me* or *WIFM?*

If your message doesn't quickly detail <u>what</u> you do and the <u>value</u> you can provide to your prospect, then don't bother reaching out. Why? Well, if you are prospecting a top target account or buyer, you only get so many chances to make a good impression before you are muted by the prospect. You can certainly hone your skills and practice on your Tier 3 accounts, but always, always put yourself in their shoes and ask yourself, WIFM?

13

EMAIL MESSAGING FRAMEWORK

A t some point in the last ten years, clients stopped answering as many phone calls as they did before. It felt as if it happened so suddenly. Almost like they were answering my calls one day, and the next day, they weren't. Obviously, some of my feelings were more emotionally driven due to feeling rejected, but there was some truth to it.

I started asking my current customers if they ever answered their desk phone, and the answer was somewhat surprising. Most said they did, but only if they recognized the number. At one point, I sat in a customer's office and watched his phone ring non-stop while we laughed together. He knew that each and every caller was a salesperson. He picked up one call and told them to call back after his meeting with me. It was one of my competitors. At this point, I started really paying attention to other communication mediums.

Email has become one of the primary sources of sales outreach for salespeople around the world. It can be a slippery slope as many salespeople, myself included at times, use it as a crutch and a reason to avoid the phone.

Nonetheless, email messaging is absolutely critical to success in sales. Regardless of what you sell, nearly everyone that has buying authority spends a large portion of their day in front of a computer or on their smartphone answering and sending emails.

In 2010, I started studying the emails logged in our CRM of the successful sellers before me, one being my mentor. My ability to craft compelling and concise emails has had a major effect on my success over the last ten years. In large organizations, it may be, or may seem, nearly impossible to reach an executive by phone. That's by design. However, if you can learn the proper framework and how to write effective and compelling emails, you'll fill your calendar with new appointments with real buyers.

As I write this, I can't help but feel how ironic it is as so much has changed in 2020 due to the COVID-19 pandemic. As a seller, you should never fear the phone or, during this unique time, video. Voice and video are the two best tools in your tool belt. They allow you to create an emotional connection to another human that is quite difficult through the written word. Given the COVID-19 pandemic, many prospects and clients are yearning for more face-to-face human action, so please take the opportunity to differentiate yourself and make that call or send that video sales call to a prospect. With that said, email will likely be a primary sales tool for years to come. Pandemic or not, your ability to master this skill will drastically increase your sales results.

Email Value Messaging Framework

Email messages are broken down into *five* key components:

1. The Subject Line

- Attention-grabbing, tied to the outcome,

something sticky (3-4 words have the highest open rates)

- If you are selling B2B in the SBM or Enterprise Marketplace, refrain from using sneaky marketing tactics to increase open rates. You aren't a snake oil salesperson, so *do not* try to trick your customers. I have tested many of these methods with not only poor results but also irritated prospects and customers. Always be ethical and honest!

2. The What

- This is what you and/or your company do that is laser specific to a business outcome or priority.
- One to two sentences *max* (One is best).

3. The Value/Credibility Statement

- What your service or product has done to drive an extremely valuable business outcome for others.
- If you can, reference clients in their industry by name or brand, recognizable adjectives are helpful. If you can't, use generalized statements such as: "We are helping 5 large financial institutions in the greater Chicago area with..."
- *Do not* focus on features of your product or service, instead focus on the business outcome you solve.

4. The Permission to Ask Close

- Assumptively ask for permission to set up the meeting or what works equally as well as if they have *interest* in a discussion.

- You can alternatively assume the meeting and split test the permission ask/interest vs. the assumptive close—I encourage you to do so!
- This is a great way to remove defense barriers and be assumptive but also extremely polite.
- You don't seem like a pushy salesperson trying to hit their quota.
- I've seen incredible results with this method.

5. The Accountable Follow Up

- We all need to be held accountable, this includes prospects and customers.
- Tell the prospect that you are going to follow up with them via phone at a very specific date and time.
- Important: This only works if you do one thing. You must *follow up* at that exact day and time! Why? Even if you don't reach the prospect, you are still in the sales cycle. Prospecting is just as much a science as it is an art. Oftentimes, prospects want to see that you are different. If you show extreme integrity by doing exactly what you say you are going to do, then they are more likely to take your next call, respond to your email, meet with you, and eventually buy from you! Always lead with integrity.

Email Example:
    (Subject Line) Prevent GDPR Compliance Fines

"Jim,

(The What) *We help clients in the financial services industry gain compliance with data privacy regulations in the EU.* (Value Credibility Statement) *More specifically, we have helped XYZ companies in the banking industry from having to pay over $1B in financial penalties prior to being audited.* ---

(Permission to Ask) *With this in mind, I'd like to ask your permission to schedule a meeting with you to understand your priorities and if you have similar challenges.*

(Accountable Close) *I'll follow up with you by phone on Wednesday (Date) at 3 pm if I've not heard back from you yet.*

Sincerely,

Erik"

Grabbing and Keeping Their Attention

As you can see, the email example above is short, to the point, and drives attention to what matters most to a prospect—solving their business problems.

If you are wondering what the dashes are in the second sentence of my email, they are the mobile preview cut offline. Why is this important?

Our goal is to grab the prospect's attention. Most of our prospects are extremely busy, but everyone has a smartphone. I don't know about you, but most people read their emails via their mobile device preview notification. They quickly decide whether or not to open, read, and/or flag the email for follow up.

Generally speaking, we usually only have 3-5 lines in a mobile preview setting, sometimes less. In those few lines, we need to use a message that immediately grabs the prospect's attention and generates enough interest that they want to read the email.

Once the prospect has opened your email, you've already

cracked the door open. Now is when the rest of your message becomes important. While you can test different strategies with different audiences, remember, generally speaking, in your initial attempts long copy (lengthy copywriting) is generally not your best route to gaining a prospect's attention. They are busy and bombarded with lengthy sales copy via email automation software.

You need to stand out from the crowd, get to the point by delivering a clear and concise message that explains what's in it for your prospect to respond to you, and take time out of their day to meet you whether that's virtually or in person. Prospecting requires salespeople to consistently test.

As a reminder, in the chapter on Sales Cadence, I wrote quite a bit about *split testing* different approaches and sales cadences. This is also equally important in your messaging. You may not land the big fish on the bait you thought you would, so you must test multiple different topics over time in your sales cadence. Even if you've done your research, it's unrealistic to believe that you'll nail the exact message your prospect is looking for the first time, every time. But we have to give it our best effort each time.

Too often, businesses and salespeople looking to grow their business claim that nothing is working, when in reality, they haven't put forth enough effort nor have they tested any two approaches for a long enough period of time to claim anything is working or isn't working. Document what is working and then leverage that information to get in front of other decision-makers and stakeholders inside your target accounts.

14

LIVE PHONE MESSAGING FRAMEWORK

The framework approach to a live prospecting call is similar to an email or voicemail with one major difference: you are speaking to a human being, This can be incredibly unpredictable and scary for many people, especially when they are unprepared and under-practiced.

With this being the case, I will cover the framework I've used, along with many other top producing sales executives, to land thousands of meetings with executives down to key informative influencers inside of large, medium, and small companies.

With this framework, we have some high-level goals we want to achieve:

1. Gain commitment and secure the meeting.
2. Differentiate ourselves from our competitors.
3. Increase positioning and interest.
4. Prevent the client from canceling the meeting.

If you are used to going for the kill the minute the prospect shows weakness, this approach feels very odd and slow. I'm not suggesting that we go at a snail's pace forever through the sales cycle, but if we can set up the foundation for our relationship with the prospect and the deal, things can accelerate rapidly throughout the sales cycle for numerous reasons with plenty of benefits. Too often, when salespeople get the slightest notion that the prospect shows interest, they attempt to set the meeting immediately. While I can understand why this is trained by many organizations, in my opinion, these same reps have many meeting cancellations due to low-value calls. This has a negative impact on the continual flow of new opportunities into a pipeline and has a drastic impact on the psychology of a seller.

Live prospecting calls can be broken down into the following segments. While they happen rather quickly, the key is to move through them with smooth transitions while pausing to actively listen to the prospect and gather information to be used to gain commitment and set-up future steps in the sales cycle.

1. The Introduction
2. Problem Statement
3. The Big Question
4. Value Prop Story
5. Pattern Interruption Assumption
6. The Summary Lockdown

1. The Introduction

Whether you've been selling for a while or are just starting out, you probably recognize that how we introduce ourselves in the first few seconds of a phone call is extremely important. Too often, salespeople use very weak introductions that start off the call in a bad position, and it's downhill from there. It's important to use language that packs a powerful punch and immediately grabs the prospect's attention and generates interest.

It's always been critically important to remember that I'm purposely interrupting my prospect in the middle of their day to ask them to give me more time in the future to have a longer discussion. We must realize that the person on the other end of the phone call was focused on something prior to our call. They also most likely don't know us, so they aren't interested in small talk.

Here are a few examples of weak introductions, along with replacements. While I have used the below introductions for years, I've also seen John Barrows share this content many times as well. I'd like to appropriately give credit where it is due and recognize a mutually shared approach to sales prospecting.

I strongly encourage you to refrain from starting off a call by saying, "Hi, may I speak to John Smith?" or "Hi, is this John?" Most of my friends address me by my first name and open up a call with "Hey, Erik!" They never open with "Hi, may I speak to Erik?" or "Hi, is this Erik Fisher?" It's almost always salespeople or telemarketers who address me with the latter. When someone opens this way, it's an immediate red flag that I've just taken a sales call.

Weak: *How are you doing today?*

Stronger: *Thanks for taking my call today.*

The weak introduction assumes that the person wants to chit chat. You've just interrupted them, and now you are asking them how they are doing. While it may seem intuitive to start a call off with a polite and conversational opening question, it's extremely awkward because they don't know you and it doesn't get to the point.

The strong introduction is still polite and gets straight to the point. It shows that you are a professional who respects their time.

Weak: *Did I catch you at a bad time?*

Stronger: *Do you have just a few minutes/moments?*

The weak introduction is something many salespeople have gotten wrong for many years. I've incorrectly used this introduction myself in the past. It rarely starts the call off on the right foot. When you ask the prospect if it's a bad time, of course, it is! You've just interrupted them. It's never a good time for a prospect to take a call from someone they don't know. They have no idea why you are calling or how much of their time they are going to waste.

The strong introduction is much better because it specifically qualifies what we are asking for, time, and quantifies how much time, minutes/moments, so the prospect can wrap their mind around what you are looking for. Most people have a few minutes, so lead with this intro instead.

Weak: *I'm just touching base,* or *I'm just checking in.*

Stronger: *The reason for my call is...*

The weak introduction holds zero value. Nearly all sales reps, including myself, have used this extremely weak introduction at some point in their career. It's one of the worst introductions to any conversation, regardless of the medium. When you call to touch base or check in with the prospect, it's not only annoying because nearly every sales rep on Earth does it, but more importantly, when you are just touching base, it means there was no reason for your call. You've now completed a double whammy no-no in sales prospecting. You interrupted the prospect and are now wasting their time for no reason. Our prospects are busy—don't waste their time.

The strong introduction is much more powerful because you are telling your prospect that you called for a very specific reason and get right to the point. It's important that you don't follow up the reason for your call with, "I'm checking in," as that's just as detrimental. Your reason for calling should be tied to a researched and known business problem that other people or businesses with similar personas are trying to solve that your offer, product, or service helps solve.

Weak: *I'm sorry to bother you.*

Stronger: *Can you help me?* or *Can you point me in the right direction?*

The weak introduction starts off the call with a negative tone. So, you've just interrupted a prospect, and now you've acknowledged that your call is a bother to them. This introduction does zero for us in getting our prospect's attention. Why would anyone want to talk to someone who is going to bother them?

The stronger introduction is great for decision-makers but also for gatekeepers. I like this introduction because humans have a natural instinct to want to help others. Helping others makes us feel good. So when we ask the prospect or gatekeeper to help us, we are stimulating a part of their brain called the supramarginal gyrus.[1] This part of the brain is responsible for empathy and compassion.

Neuroscience also tells us that when we help others, the neurochemical *oxytocin* is released, which is one of the three neurochemicals called the *Happiness Trifecta,* which gives us a boost in mood.[2] When we ask our prospects for help, we are stimulating these parts of the brain, which plays in our favor.

I do need to warn you not to overuse the "Can you help me?" introduction. It can be misread as disingenuous and dishonest if you know you are speaking to the prospect you were looking for. I've used this introduction many times in my career with much success and have never had anyone tell me they felt it was dishonest; however, Christopher Voss, author of *Never Split the Difference* and former head of FBI Hostage Negotiations, claims that it can instantly start the conversation off on the wrong foot if used incorrectly.[3]

In my experience, asking for help is a great way to leverage psychology and break down walls when we are looking for *some help* to get to the decision-maker or validating that we have the correct person on the phone.

My typical introduction goes something like this:

Hi Prospect First Name,
Thanks for taking my call today.
Do you have a few minutes/moments?
Great. The reason for my call is… / Can you help me?

At this point, the prospect normally asks who I am and why I'm calling.

I then respond with: *This is Erik from (insert company), and the reason for my call is…*

2. The Problem Statement

Similar to a prospecting email, the goal of this portion of a prospecting call is to determine if your prospect has a similar problem to others in their industry or with their same persona. How we approach this needs to be to the point to catch the prospect's attention as we tie what we *do* to a very specific problem within their industry, company, or market.

As this is likely the first time we have spoken to the prospect, we don't have much time to grab their attention. To show the prospect that we value their time, we make a very specific *problem statement* that will hopefully generate enough interest and attention that they will want to continue on with the conversation.

Additionally, we want to reference data or information that we have gained through our pre-call research to establish instant credibility and differentiate ourselves.

Similar to the email example, there is no need to reinvent the wheel. As you transition out of your introduction, when your prospect asks who you are and why you are calling, you can say something similar to the following:

> *My name is Erik, and I'm with XYZ Company. The reason for my call is that many of our customers are struggling to gain compliance with new privacy laws in the EU (European Union) and are fearful of paying significant financial penalties. I understand your company does significant business in Europe and would be required to comply with the new GDPR law. We help our clients gain compliance more quickly through our data protection services.*

In this example, the *problem statement* clearly explains the problem the prospect's industry peers are facing that they are also likely facing. It also references significant financial penalties, which further generates interest for the prospect if they indeed have the same problems and concerns. We establish credibility by sharing some very public information about their company that further proves our knowledge of the challenges affecting their business.

Finally, the last statement clearly explains what our company does to help alleviate or prevent the problem.

At this point, it is imperative to pause for a brief moment

in the event that the prospect wants to respond to this problem statement. This is where many salespeople make the mistake of continuing to talk. Pause for too long, and it gets awkward; don't pause at all, and it's not a conversation. With that said, in my experience, it's best to take a short but deep breath and follow up with a strategic question tied back to your problem statement, the prospect's current situation, and the future vision.

3. The Big Question

At this point, we made a strong introduction and led with a *problem statement* along with the value our company provides to our clients in order to grab our prospect's attention. It is now time to pivot the conversation to get our prospect thinking further about their current situation. The goal of *The Big Question* is to get the prospect to not only think about their current situation but generate interest in speaking to us further once they have come to the realization that they have an actual problem that needs to be addressed or remediated via an outside party.

Let's begin by diving into the mindset we must have when we reach this step in the call.

While I label this step in the framework *The Big Question*, in a singular form, in actuality, it will be a few deep questions to further probe the prospect to validate that the prospect has already identified the problem we have called out in our problem statement but also to qualify if they deem the problem important enough to take action. Just because someone has a problem does not mean that they are ready to take action to solve it. We need to be keenly aware of prospects who may say yes to a meeting with us but end up wasting our time. As salespeople, we should look to disqualify prospects instead of attempting to persuade them or qualify them into our business.

At this step in our sales process, we are not looking to solve the prospect's problem. Too often, this is a huge mistake that salespeople make in an initial call. I've made this mistake myself in the past as it's the way most salespeople are wired. The minute the prospect confirms that they have a similar problem to their industry peers, we want to dive headfirst into solving the problem and start closing them. It's actually quite natural for us to want to solve, solve, solve. We need to slow down and stop this behavior. We don't have nearly enough information, and the prospect often has not bought into the significance of their problem nor our ability to solve it.

I love the doctor analogy here. How would you feel if your doctor immediately started prescribing you medication without first diagnosing your symptoms and the root cause? I hope you'd run out of the office as fast as you could. Imagine how our prospects feel when we start recommending and selling before we diagnose the issue. While this example can be used throughout many early steps in the sales process, it's a great example of what we shouldn't do on a first sales prospecting call.

In addition to not jumping the gun on solving the prospect's problem, the goal of the first prospecting call is also not to go through a lengthy phone meeting with the prospect where you engage in a series of planned discovery questions. Sure, keep the conversation going if the prospect is engaged but just be aware and cautious of where you are with the person on the other end of the call.

In my experience, prospects go through multiple iterations of AIDA. They first went through AIDA when they decided to take action to meet with you. They may go through the AIDA process many more times consecutively or separately as they are moved through the sales funnel. Prospects are constantly at war with emotional and rational decision making. They often bounce back and forth in their belief and trust in their decision and the impact it will have on themselves first and their business second.

As we engage in the first call, if all works out well, we will have solidified a scheduled meeting on the prospect's calendar when both the seller and the prospect can properly prepare for the meeting. This is important for three major reasons:

First, it allows the prospect to clearly think about their problem, the desired future state, if they have a desire to fix their problem, and finally, how they will go about resolving it.

Secondly, scheduling a planned meeting lets the salesperson do more research on the prospect and prepare well thought-out questions to gather relevant information in the discovery meeting to be used throughout the sales process to diagnose the problem and make an appropriate recommendation. While there is some light discovery questioning that takes place to gain a micro-commitment from the prospect prior to the first scheduled meeting, it is imperative to be well prepared to ask deep, probing questions and engage in a meaningful conversation where you are both building rapport and also determining if the prospect is the right fit for you and your business and vice versa.

Lastly, when we get a micro-commitment from the prospect in the form of a scheduled meeting, it reduces the number of meeting cancellations and future back-outs in the sales process. If we are honest with ourselves, we have all had prospects and clients cancel meetings with us. Some of them reschedule, but many prospects disappear into the darkness, never to be heard from again. Many salespeople and business owners are mystified as to why this happens. It's unfortunate that this happens in sales, but you can reduce this from happening if your initial call is handled properly.

Prospects change their minds often due to many variables, but often, it's because they were rushed and didn't have time to clearly think through the initial discussion. The human brain has a hard time refocusing when we are interrupted. This is further compounded by the fact that we only retain a very small amount of what we hear. There has been significant research on this very topic.

According to a Harvard Business Review article titled, "Listening to People," by Ralph G. Nichols and Leonard A. Stevens,[4] "immediately after the average person has listened to someone talk, he remembers only about half of what he has heard—no matter how carefully he thought he was listening."

Nichols and Stevens go on to write, "In general, people feel that concentration while listening is a greater problem than concentration during any other form of personal communication. Actually, listening concentration is more difficult."

When we apply the findings from this research to our initial sales call, a few things come to light:

1. Within eight hours, prospects will have forgotten one-half to one-third of what was discussed.
2. Prospects have trouble retaining what they hear in a conversation as we have interrupted them.
   Listening concentration is more difficult than just concentration alone.

The point of referencing the above research findings is to simply help us understand that we can't expect our prospects to remember the majority of what we discussed in an initial call or even a scheduled meeting. When you combine the *forgetful factor* mentioned above with the fact that we've interrupted a prospect, along with the fact that most of our prospects are bombarded with new distractions and things they need to get done, the chances that we will have a call that is both informative and memorable are slim.

It is for this reason that we focus our initial prospecting call on scheduling a planned meeting. At that time, we engage in prepared conversational discovery, perhaps sharing visuals in person, which have been shown to drastically improve retention rates. These benefits will help us as we move through our sales process with the prospect.

At this time, I'd like to point out that the advice I provided above is directed towards sellers who are in more strategic and complex sales. Transactional-based sales may require much shorter sales cycles and even closing off of the first or second call; however, there are still benefits to slowing things down to speed up your results in the long run.

Let's now dive into the nuts and bolts of *The Big Question.*

As we have just made our problem statement, it's now most logical to move onto a simple question to gain confirmation that the client agrees that they too have the same or similar problem or desired outcome.

The simplest way to ask this question is in an open-ended format to get the prospect to either agree or disagree and elaborate on their answers. We want to refrain from closed-ended questions at this point. The more we get the prospect to open up to us and do the talking, the better.

Example:

Based on the information I provided, can you elaborate on your business or situation and how these challenges are affecting you and/or your company? or How are these issues affecting your business?

In these examples, the prospect could respond in a variety of ways. You will likely get one of three responses in some form or fashion:

1. I'm not interested / I'm already engaged with another partner to help us.
2. We are experiencing similar issues... (Prospect elaborates on the issue in more specific detail.)
3. We don't have that problem.

It's not to say that you won't get a few bad apples that will hit you with the short and sharp, "I'm not interested," reply, but if you've made it this far, they've stayed on the phone for a reason. In my experience, very few prospects who have stayed on the phone this long actually respond this way.

At this point, it is your job to keenly listen to the prospect's response to decipher what they are really saying. Many times, this is difficult. Prospects can be short on the phone and don't openly share information, which makes it hard to know where they are really at. If we take everything we hear at surface level, many great opportunities will pass us by.

4. The Value Prop Story

If you recall, we already made our value proposition when we led with our problem statement. This is where most salespeople struggle. Many salespeople have been trained that the "pitch" is where the money is made. Do you like being pitched on something? Can you tell when someone is pitching? I'm sure you can. So can your prospects. Nobody likes being pitched anything, so don't do it. Instead of pitching them on how great we are and why they should work with us, we want to lead with an approach that interrupts the prospect's patterns.

Most salespeople take this opportunity to pitch the prospect on amazing features and benefits of their product or service. To interrupt this pattern of conditioning, we want to ask our prospect if we can summarize what we've heard back to them to make sure we've understood their problem at this point in the call. This accomplishes a few things:

1. Continues to reduce defense barriers.
2. Shows the prospect we are actually listening to them.
3. Flushes out discrepancies in our understanding.
4. Allows the prospect to elaborate further.
5. Increases the potential for the prospect to ask for the meeting themselves.

Here's an example of what this would look like:

Seller: "John, thanks for sharing the current state of your business. To make sure I understand your business problem clearly at this point, would it be okay to quickly summarize what I've heard?"

Prospect: "Sure, go ahead."

Seller: "You shared that your biggest concern is the lack of security controls in place and the sheer amount of data shared globally across the organization is hard to wrap your arms around to determine your level of risk.

Additionally, you are unsure of the best route to take to put governance around your data and the access people have to this data internally and externally.

Lastly, and most importantly, if you aren't able to secure and classify the data, your privacy office will be knocking at your door because the organization will be at risk of a significant multi-million dollar financial penalty. And this all needs to be completed by May 30th.

John, does that cover it?"

Prospect: "Yes, that's exactly it!"

Seller: "Ok, thanks for confirming my understanding."

If you misheard any part of your prospect's problem, the prospect will likely correct you and add in the parts you missed or misunderstood. This is a great benefit because you can document additional key information that you will use in future steps in your sales process.

While this may or may not be a more sophisticated sales scenario than what you are used to, you can apply this to nearly any prospecting call. The approach and framework will be similar, but the data and issues will be different, maybe less financially driven, and the problems and drivers will be more personal. The thing is, in this scenario, this situation seems financially driven on the surface, *avoiding a potentially crippling financial penalty,* but more than that, it is likely very personal. What if our prospect, John, could lose his job if things don't go as he needs them to?

You have a decision to make at this point, you can follow up your comments with additional questions or move into your value statement.

The purpose of asking additional questions is to really pull out the root cause and driving factor for change. In this scenario, it's both saving the company from paying a substantial financial penalty and potentially also saving John's job. Obviously, if you can have that kind of impact on someone's career, you have a solid anchor to hold your deal tight throughout the sales process.

The good news is that many deals, while rational on the surface, are also very emotionally driven and personal, which is one major reason why decision making in business-to-business sales is spread across many different people. Nobody wants to take the blame, so they share it!

It is up to you as a salesperson to feel out the call and the prospect's willingness to share information on whether or not this is the appropriate time and necessary to "drag them through the glass" and feel their pain.

If you feel that you've established rapport quickly, and the prospect has been sharing information pretty freely, then you can ask the following.

Seller: "John, I don't want to make any assumptions here, but what happens if your company ends up paying the fine?"

The inflection and tonality you use when you ask this question is critically important. Think of how you'd ask a friend or loved one about how something troubling is impacting them personally. You can be professional, polite, and very business oriented while coming from a place of authenticity. The prospect may not only open up to you, helping you anchor yourself to a must-solve problem, but you will further build rapport, which makes closing the deal much easier in the long run. Always be genuine. By doing so, you'll show up differently. You'll be surprised by what people are willing to share with you.

A majority of sales training I've been through and most of the books I've read encourage the salesperson to ask an additional question. In most cases, I encourage it, but I must warn you, you need to read the person and situation to determine if it's the right time to push a little further. Not all situations are equal. This is where the art of sales becomes important.

At this juncture in the call, we've arrived at another danger zone for most salespeople. In our example, let's assume we made the decision to ask John the next question. He shares with us that he will indeed be at risk of being fired if his company can't gain compliance quickly enough and ends up paying the large financial penalty. Of course, we need to ask for a meeting. If we don't ask in sales, we never get anywhere, but we aren't there yet.

Don't jump the gun and say, "John, I think it's imperative we meet as soon as possible. We've helped numerous other customers in the same situation you are in, and I'm sure we can help!"

There's a better way. We've created attention, we've created interest, and we have an overall confirmed understanding of the business problem and the emotional drivers behind it. We've also created urgency by asking the additional follow-up question. Why not ask for the meeting? Well, we could. Or we could be a bit different.

We will use a value statement through storytelling that will leave the prospect feeling as though we are a credible partner to work with. We aren't sure that we are the right fit for their business needs until we discuss this further, but we have helped other people drive results through our product or solution.

Seller: "John, based on what you've shared, you are showing many of the same symptoms and business problems some of our other customers have also encountered.

We recently helped a customer in the financial industry that was also struggling to gain compliance to prevent costly GDPR fines. This customer has 80% of their business in Europe, so it was an absolute necessity for them to secure their data as quickly as possible while improving their policies. We were able to accomplish this with them in less than four months, and they have now gained 100% compliance as of their last audit.

John, at this point, I'd like to learn some more specifics about your business and challenges. I'm not sure that we are the right partner to help you yet, as there is additional information we'd need to understand to determine that.

With that said, would you like to learn more about the process we go through to help customers so we can determine if we should continue?"

Prospect: "Yes."

In this storytelling value statement, we led with:

- Peer relatability: Prospect is not alone; we've seen this before.
- Story: We helped another customer with a similar scenario with the focus on the *result*.
- Pattern Interrupt: They are used to the seller

telling them they are the right fit! We will diagnose the problem further.

- Qualification Question: Determine if the prospect is ready to make a *decision* to take the next step. This is both a qualification question and a micro-commitment question.

We now transition into the close, or as I call it, Pattern Interruption Assumption, where we continue to interrupt the pattern the prospect is used to.

5. Pattern Interruption Assumption

Similar to our email messaging framework, we need to assumptively ask the prospect to "close" them on taking our meeting. At this point, this is where most salespeople fail. If you don't ask, you'll never get what you desire in sales or in life.

You can assumptively ask the prospect when they have availability to meet in the next few days or weeks, which I've seen much success with in my career. It's easy, and it works great. However, I like the idea of continually leveraging multiple strategies in a cohesively bundled approach, which almost always ends with a booked meeting.

The purpose and reasoning for what may seem like a lengthy sales messaging framework up to this point is to generate ultimate credibility and create value. This makes closing the prospect on taking our meeting as simple as possible and prevents future hiccups in the sales cycle.

If we look back at the AIDA buyer process, we have caught the prospect's attention, continued to generate interest, and have determined the prospect has made the decision to take the next step in the process in meeting with us.

The next step in a buyer's thought process is to take

action. Many times earlier in my career, I'd get nervous, rush off the phone, and tell the prospect that I'd send over some times, and they can get back to me with a time that works for them. Of course, this may seem polite and non-pushy, but too often, the prospect gets busy and never returns your email as it is buried amongst the rest of the noise in their inbox. We have to take the opportunity to schedule the meeting when their interest and attention level has peaked.

Our prospects' interest and action-taking levels decrease as time passes. You may be the first salesperson to call the prospect, yet an hour after your call, a smarter sales rep calls your prospect and books the meeting on the spot. You are long forgotten.

In order to prevent this from happening, take a two-pronged approach that includes simply using assumptive close questions paired with another pattern interruption to schedule the meeting.

Before we look at how we leverage the assumptive close and pattern interruption, let's quickly look at what we are trying to accomplish with each tactic.

The assumptive close question's purpose is to accomplish four things:

1. Determine urgency
2. Determine other decision-makers and influencers involved
3. Make it easier on our prospect to take action
4. Schedule the meeting ASAP

The pattern interruption's purpose is to:

1. Continue to interrupt the pattern of thinking the prospect has developed from conversations with other sellers
2. Removes the fear of rejection

3. Differentiate ourselves from our competitors
4. Make our conversation and ourselves more memorable in the eyes of the prospect
5. Leverage psychology to get a "yes" as the sales cycle continues

Examples of assumptive closing questions include:

- When does it make sense for us to meet for a deeper discussion?
- Can you pull up your calendar and tell me what days and times you are open for an hour meeting next week?
- Who else should we invite to our meeting?
- Is there anything that would prevent us from meeting next week at _____ or _____?

As you can see, these are all simple assumptive questions. Pick one and test it out to see what you are most comfortable with and what provides the best results for you.

Unfortunately, most people shy away from asking in this fashion because they feel they are being pushy. I can assure you that you are not. Always ask, all the time. If you did the upfront work as described in this book, you should feel very confident that they need to meet with you, so there is no need to shy away from this.

The assumptive close question works great as a stand-alone way to close and book the meeting. However, it's what we say before which greatly increases our odds of the prospect booking the meeting with us, but more importantly, sets up a much easier conversation with the prospect in the meeting and creates enormous curiosity. This is where pattern interruption comes into play again.

How often do you think our prospects have a salesperson preface their closing statement with "I'm not sure if our solution/product is for you"? If you think almost never, then you are spot on!

After years and years of conversations with prospects and clients, many of them have shared with me that most salespeople tell them they can solve all their problems or their product/service is the perfect fit for them. Usually after the first call or first meeting.

How could you possibly determine that so quickly when you haven't yet done any discovery on a prospect, their problem, or the political landscape? You may not even want them as your client in the end, so don't put yourself or your prospect in that scenario so quickly.

Secondly, do you want your prospect to trust you? It's like any relationship; trust is built over time. While we all have sales targets to hit, I can tell you that the fastest way to the top is to slow down to speed up. Build trust and be different than your competitors by being authentic and genuine. You may feel that your solution is the perfect fit for them, and you may be correct, but your prospect probably isn't emotionally, logically, or psychologically there yet.

In order to change up the prospect's pattern of thinking, we want to make a statement that disarms them and psychologically encourages them to want to discuss their problem and our solution more in the future. Additionally, we will greatly differentiate ourselves by being the complete opposite of pushy while simultaneously assuming the close to book the meeting.

Lastly, what we say matters more than you think. Let's look at an example of interrupting a pattern while using an assumptive close to encourage the prospect to take action and want to book the meeting right then and there.

As I mentioned, most prospects are conditioned to expect a salesperson to make some statement that alludes to their product or solution being the perfect fit for solving their business problem or reaching their desired outcome.

Instead, what we will say flips the script upside down.

Seller: "At this point, while it seems that you have a problem or situation that we have helped other customers solve, I'm not sure this is right for you yet, but we can usually determine if it's a mutual fit after another discussion where we dive a bit deeper into your problem. When does it make sense for us to meet again next week to discuss this further?"

Let's break this down.

At this point, while it seems that you have a problem or situation that we have helped other customers solve,

This continues with our theme of credibility and relevance.

I'm not sure if this is right for you yet,

If you fear being rejected, this is one of the best ways to overcome this fear while also creating a no-pressure situation for your prospect. Since the prospect is used to people telling them how great their product/solution is and that it is right for them, this immediately drops their defense barriers and reduces stress for them to make it easier to take action on scheduling the meeting. You are showing the prospect that you aren't making any assumptions about what you think you know about their problem. You are also setting yourself up for future success because you may find out that you do not want to invest more time with this prospect after your first meeting. Lastly, history and psychology tell us that when we hear that we may not want something or it may not be for us, it creates a burning desire to find out if we want it or if it is right for us.

but we can usually determine a mutual fit after another discussion after we dive a bit deeper into your problem.

Think about this scenario: your boss tells you how great a job you've been doing in growing your sales territory and hitting your sales numbers, *but* they would like to see you spend more time in the office helping others. You will likely only remember the last sentence of the conversation, what was said after the word "but."

Since we tend to only remember what comes after the word "but," the prospect will focus on your ask for the next meeting, the outcome you may be able to deliver, and should open their calendar to schedule the meeting at that moment.

Worst case scenario: The prospect says they need some time to think it over, but the chances of them responding when you follow up are much higher as you have differentiated yourself.

When does it make sense for us to meet again next week to discuss this further?

We've now transitioned into our assumptive close question. The secret sauce behind the way we ask is that we make the prospect feel that we are putting the power and control back in their hands by asking when it makes sense for them to meet and giving them our availability. By assuming they want to meet with us, providing a specific time or time frame of the meeting, in actuality, we are still in control of the conversation but leading them to take the action we want.

It is important at this point to ask the prospect to pull up their calendar and together schedule a time to meet for the next step. Encouraging this action will be helpful to you and your prospect. Delaying them from taking action at that moment is a critical mistake. You've taken the time to bring a heightened sense of awareness to the pain their problem is causing or the interest in the desired future state they wish to reach. If you wait until a later date, the need to take action may pass as other priorities come into play.

When the prospect provides a time slot they are available, you need to be aware of the psychology behind availability. While anyone in sales can understand how difficult it is to book solid meetings with new prospects, being too available is never a good thing. Being completely unavailable doesn't work either. Take the time to schedule a solid 30-45 minute meeting when you know you'll be ready, not rushed from another meeting, and can make a solid impression on your potential future client. Telling you to turn down the first time slot provided isn't really great advice as each situation is different, so use your best judgment. If you seem too available and the prospect asks you to meet the very next morning, I recommend that you share that you are booked the rest of the day and want to take some time to prepare for the meeting, so that the discussion is valuable for both parties and politely recommend a few alternate times.

Once you've scheduled the meeting, one of my favorite follow-up questions to ask is: *Who else is this topic relevant to that we should include in the conversation?*

This is intended to bring as many relevant people to the table that have influence, opinion, or decision-making authority over the purchasing decision so that they don't appear later on in the sales cycle and stall or slow the deal from being closed.

As you are bringing this question to the table, the prospect may either suggest the names and roles of others in the organization you'll send the calendar invite to or in some cases, they may want to meet with you on their own first to establish more rapport and ensure they trust you before bringing others into the fold. Either way, this is a great way to be thoughtful, proactive, and show your prospect that you have been through many engagements before and understand that there are likely others involved.

Your question may come up on its own as a small objection you'll need to address when you ask for the meeting. The prospect may state that they need to talk to others who are involved to check their schedules. If so, that's a good thing. While it may feel like an objection to stall scheduling the meeting, as stated before, I encourage others with influence or a vested interest in the buying decision to join. In this case, I suggest agreeing with the prospect, sharing that it's a great idea, and sharing that you were going to suggest the same. If they still stall and say they need to talk to others before scheduling, you can tackle this in numerous ways. What I suggest and what happens to work 90% of the time is the following:

Ask the person to pull up their colleagues' calendars to check their availability. If available, you can send the meeting invitation to all parties with a summary of the purpose of the meeting. You can even include a message stating, "John thought it would be a great idea to invite you to our discussion; we hope to see you there." Then you simply need to ask the prospect to follow up with their partners to fill them in on the purpose of the meeting. Lastly, be sure to get the full names, role titles, and email addresses before ending the conversation so you can be well-prepared and do research on the attendees prior to the meeting.

6. The Summary Lockdown

In 2009, I was in my first full year selling to a mid-market B2B sales territory. While I was green in B2B sales, I had several years of B2C sales under my belt and thought I knew how to message effectively and handle objections. However, I started noticing a frustrating trend. After booking my calendar full of twelve to fifteen solid appointments, one of two scenarios kept rearing its ugly head. Either my meeting canceled at the last minute as I was preparing to walk out the door, or equally frustrating, when I arrived, the prospect wasn't prepared for our conversation and had forgotten what the purpose of the meeting was.

This is not only frustrating for the salesperson, it also means we wasted the prospect's time on the phone leading up to the meeting. If the meeting didn't cancel, we would have to spend more time going back to the drawing board reminding the prospect of our conversation, the problem they shared with us, and why it was of value for them to meet with us. I'm not a fan of wasting my time nor my prospect's time. We are all busy and need to be as efficient as possible.

If this has happened to you, you're not alone. It happens to thousands of salespeople daily, but it's not without a solution. One of the best ways I've found to further lock the prospect down on our meeting and ensure they are prepared for a valuable conversation is what I call The Summary Lockdown.

This strategy is one that I've used for the greater part of the last five years with much success. I rarely have meetings cancel on me, and if they do, they almost always to reschedule. I also almost always have prospects that are primed and ready for a mutually beneficial conversation in order to maintain control of the conversation and advance the prospect to the next step in the sales cycle.

The Summary Lockdown is simply an email we send the prospect no later than the close of business on the day we book the meeting. Sounds pretty simple, right? That's because it is simple! However, to maximize its value, it must be properly executed.

The email has five components in a specific order outlined below:

1. Gratitude
2. Confirmation
3. Summary

4. **Engagement Clarification**
5. **Follow-Up**

Example:

Steve,

Thanks for spending a few moments on the phone with me today. (Gratitude) As discussed, we have scheduled a conversation in your office on Date/Time to discuss your ongoing challenges with GDPR compliance. (Confirmation)

Below is a summary of top points you made during our discussion today. If you can, please come prepared for our meeting with any relevant information and required capabilities you need in a partner so we can determine if we are a good fit for each other. I will equally come prepared to make the most of our time together. (Summary)

Summary:

- *Data Privacy Issues due to lack of security controls*
- *Data classification issues*
- *Hard date of May 30th to become compliant*
- *Lack of compliance could result in significant financial penalties (Summary)*

If there is anything I missed in my summary, please let me know, and I'll make sure to address this in our time together. (Engagement/Clarification)

I will follow up with you by phone and email two days before our appointment to re-confirm. (Follow-Up)

Best Regards,

Erik

Each component in our email has a purpose. In sales, while it's important to not be robotic and overly scripted, it is important that we do most things with intentful purpose.

Gratitude: When we show gratitude, we warm the prospect up and ensure they know we appreciate their time and don't take it for granted.

Confirmation: When we confirm our meeting, we take the opportunity to remind the client again of the date and time of our meeting and the main topic we are discussing.

Summary: We show the prospect we were actively listening during our conversation and understand their problems and goals. Furthermore, knowledge is power. It's important that we share what we heard in our discussion so that we can verify we heard the prospect correctly.

Engagement and Clarification: Coming off the last step of summarizing our meeting, we take the opportunity to ensure the prospect is engaged by subtly asking them to review our summary and correct or confirm what we heard in our discussion.

Follow-Up: Lastly, we let the prospect know that we will be calling them at a specific date to reconfirm our time together to ensure that nothing has changed. This is imperative to becoming a highly efficient salesperson who doesn't waste time.

The majority of salespeople rely on email as their sole method of prospecting new accounts and the stakeholders within. While relying solely on email is entirely wrong and will lead to less than desirable results, it is still a critical tool in our prospecting tool belt that is important to master. By following the framework outlined in this chapter, you'll be well on your way to achieving a calendar full of appointments with new prospects and existing customers. Better yet, when mastered, you'll need far less attempts to reach tough decision makers that only elite salespeople can reach, putting you in the ultimate position to fill your funnel with more opportunities, resulting in more sales and more income!

Building Momentum Action Step

Now is the time to ensure that you are taking steps to use The Intelligence Factor to your advantage! Go to your *Ready. Aim. Fire Workbook* and complete the exercises and questions for Part III. Within the workbook, complete a current cadence analysis, assess your past communication medium usage, and practice split-testing with your sales cadence to identify what is and isn't working.

To access your complimentary *Ready. Aim. Fire Workbook,* go to www.TheIntelligenceFactor.com/freeworkbook

PART IV

PROSPERING THROUGH PROSPECTING

15

CALLING WITH CONFIDENCE

A s you read through the prior chapters, you may have felt that the phone messaging approach I suggest seems to lack confidence as we aren't immediately jumping in to solve problems, even when we are sure we can fix them. Quite the contrary. In fact, confidence in ourselves, our product/service, and our ability to diagnose a problem is why we follow a solution-minded approach which seeks understanding first, solutions last. Understand that the best salespeople have the utmost confidence in themselves, and this shows in their sales calls.

When you begin to master the sales skills needed to be successful, true confidence is displayed through a calm, natural, and confident rhythm in a sales call. The tone and pace of a confident seller's approach comes through on the phone.

We've all rushed through a sales call at some point in our career. When I've rushed a call, it's because I was usually unprepared and under-practiced, which led to a severe lack of confidence. The sooner I could get off a call, the better because I wasn't prepared for the unknown. When practiced and prepared, you'll have a better sense of the tonality, pace, and flow of a conversation with a prospect. When you know what question to ask next and how to pivot, your confidence will soar and your pipeline will thank you. Finally, before you jump into making some calls, let's cover some incredibly helpful tips that will increase your odds of converting a cold or lukewarm prospect into a live meeting. You've probably heard these tips before, but there is a reason they've been written about and used in sales training for years. They work!

1. Stand Up

Standing improves your posture. Standing opens up your lungs, which allows you to breathe and stay calm. Phone calls rely heavily on voice tonality and inflection. Your prospects are imagining what you look like when they hear your voice. Standing up greatly improves both tonality and inflection.

When you stand, you sound more confident, and all human beings like engaging with people who are confident. This does not mean arrogant; nobody likes arrogant salespeople, so please know the difference between an arrogant, pushy salesperson vs. a confident, cool, calm, and collected individual who seems as if they have been there and done that a thousand times over.

Standing up improves your energy levels. When you have energy, you are more likely to be yourself and have a more dynamic, free-flowing message. You want to sound like a human being, not a robot.

2. Be Prepared

We all have a mental block every now and again; it happens to me all the time. The way to tackle this is by being prepared. If you run into a situation where you lose your train of thought due to the prospect throwing you off your rhythm, having prepared and rehearsed responses and questions to address potential objections helps get you right back into the flow of the conversation.

It's important to have some key information on hand. Having a couple of key facts about the person and company at your disposal is very helpful. It shows the prospect that you have done your research, which instantly helps you stand out from the crowd of unprepared general sales reps that call them on a daily basis. It isn't hard to acquire this information, and it can be a huge differentiator!

Lastly, have a well-rehearsed response to follow up at a specific date and time for specific reasons if you are drawing dead on the call. Never leave the call without a nailed down next step, even if they aren't interested.

3. Slow Down

There is no need to rush. Oftentimes, you will feel like you are speaking very slowly, but you're likely speaking at a perfect conversational speed. Remember, it should be a conversation; nobody likes being talked at. By speaking too quickly and trying to get through your pitch, you are overstimulating your prospects, which causes the neurons in their brain to go haywire. Overly stimulated prospects can't think clearly enough to decide if they actually want to meet with you. If you are speaking too quickly, they can't process the information.

Also, if you speak too quickly, you will appear nervous or wired. Confidence is important in all aspects of sales. Salespeople with confidence display calm, yet authoritative and friendly tonality and pace. Think about how doctors, attorneys, financial advisors, and other professionals speak to make you feel comfortable: calm, cool, friendly, and collected. They display an incredible amount of authority in their niche, which makes you want to listen to them and makes it easy for them to broach a conversation.

Leave yourself a voicemail or role play with someone else, and practice speaking at a calm pace with some energy. Listen to yourself and ask for feedback from others on your tone, inflection, and pace of speech.

4. Pause

You are having a conversation when you speak to someone on the phone, so keep it that way. When you say "Hi John," pause for a few seconds to let the other person respond. Don't interrupt your prospect. You want them to respond to you.

Pausing allows the person on the other end of the call to process the new information they've just received when you've just interrupted them in the middle of their day. Be prepared to ask for a micro-commitment or meeting. Once you ask, *pause,* and let the prospect respond with a "yes" or "no." *Remember, it's a conversation, which includes at least two people and requires you to* listen. You can't possibly be prepared to address objections if you aren't listening intently.

Lastly, pausing will calm you down if you are nervous or overstimulated. You may feel like you are pausing for an eternity. You're not, trust me. If you want to find out how your pauses sound, role play or leave yourself a voicemail. You'll be surprised how natural you sound when you listen to yourself.

5. Eliminate Distractions

This applies to nearly everything you are trying to accomplish in life and business. You can get an incredible amount of work done when you eliminate all distractions and focus on the task at hand. The world we live in today is filled with more distractions than any other time in history, largely due to the fact that we are digitally connected in so many ways.

According to research presented by Ofcom, the UK regulator of communication services, we pick up our smartphones every 12 minutes.[1] Unfortunately, most salespeople aren't picking up their phones every 12 minutes to make a call. Our phones are often distractions, rather than tools when not used deliberately.

Moreover, it has been proven that humans can accomplish far more on a daily basis when they stop multitasking and focus on one thing on their to-do list or plan at a time.

Feel like you get more accomplished when you multitask? Here's some scientific proof that you don't.

Torkel Klingberg, professor of cognitive neuroscience at the Karolinska Institutet in Sweden, wrote in his book, *The Overflowing Brain*, "attention is the portal through which the information flood reaches the brain" but that our brains lack "boundless capacity" to both pay attention and process attention.[2]

When it comes to making sales prospecting calls, you must be 100% focused and dialed into each conversation.

Turn off your email on your computer and phone. Leave text messages on as it's an efficient way to follow up with a prospect right after their call to verify you have their cell phone number stored correctly and thank them for their call. Disregard any and all text messages from friends or family, unless, of course, it's a true emergency.

6. Have Fun!

If you are selling anything, you are going to be making lots of phone calls. It's a required element of the game, so make it fun! Most people hate making prospecting calls for a host of reasons described in earlier chapters, so you might as well find creative ways to enjoy the process as you'll be spending more than half of your career making calls to prospects and customers.

Some easy ways to create a fun environment are:

Competition: Grab some colleagues and create a competition on who can set the most appointments with a small reward or bragger's rights for the day for the winner. Easy, competitive, and loads of fun.

Around the Horn: I first heard about this from a video training by John Barrows. Get a group of colleagues together for a call block and sit around a table. Each person makes a call on speakerphone while the others listen. The salesperson making the call does his best to set up a meeting and the others take notes on what went well and what didn't. After each call, the next person in the rotation makes the next call on speakerphone. This continues until the call block is over. After the call block has concluded, discuss with your group what strategies worked and what needs improvement. The key with this setup is that everyone becomes extremely vulnerable and everyone makes mistakes, so it helps get over the normal pre-call jitters. I promise you'll get some good laughs as prospects can be so unpredictable you're bound to laugh at some of the objections and rebuttals used. This environment is also great for leveraging your peers' strategies and approaches and try implementing them yourself.

Treat Yourself: This is fairly simple, but it's a nice way to reward yourself for a job well done. Think of a nice, affordable reward for hitting a goal. Could be an overpriced coffee, sweet treat, happy hour, or an article of clothing. Be wary, though, that once you start crushing it, buying yourself new clothes daily can get rather pricey. Not a bad problem to have!

Set up a call for the number of appointments or second step calls you were able to schedule. When you hit the goal at the end of your call block, reward yourself!

Whether you are a naturally confident person or not, it's critically important to practice and develop your skills as a salesperson. While there are plenty of naturally confident people in the world, if you aren't one of them, that's perfectly okay. Confidence can be developed by consistently practicing the right sales strategies and tactics. While being confident feels great on a sales call or meeting with a client, the by-product of your confidence is what really matters. Confidence is contagious. Our prospects and customers usually have enough on their plates in their personal and professional lives. Helping your clients feel at ease and more comfortable will bring clarity. They will be more confident in their choice to spend their time or money with you.

16

ADDRESSING OBJECTIONS

A s a salesperson, you cannot make progress if you do not know how to handle objections. Often, when faced with objections, we freeze and give up. Alternatively, many salespeople avoid prospecting completely because they do not want to deal with objections. You cannot gain more clients if you are uncomfortable reaching out to prospects and addressing their objections.

The Four Objections

There are four different types of objections that you need to become familiar with and prepare for. If you are aware of the variety of ways a prospect might object at specific points in the process, you can better anticipate how to address the objection and move forward.

Prospecting objections occur when you call someone, and they give you a quick negative response. It is a conditioned response to object to a sales call. It is no different than when a telemarketer calls you, and you just say, "I'm not interested," and hang up.

Micro-commitment objections occur when you ask a

prospect to move to the next step in the sales process. If you ask them if you can talk to the boss about the budget, and they resist, they are objecting to making a micro-commitment with that next step.

Left-field Objections occur when the prospect brings up an objection that is not part of the conversation you're having at that moment. They result in throwing the salesperson off from the focus on the conversation. Most salespeople end up going down a rabbit hole with the prospect when responding to this type of objection. It totally throws them of their game plan for that meeting, and they spend the entire time trying to refute that objection.

Buying or closing objections occur when you ask someone to make a purchasing decision. In B2B sales, if you've done all of the work ahead of time, you may not have this type of objection because it is clear that your product or solution fits what they're looking for.

However, when you tell someone that the next step is to sign the contract, they may object by saying, "Well, I need to go talk to my boss." Although they may feel you are the right fit, the prospect might still object to making a buying decision at that moment.

Multiple Stakeholder Objections

In B2C sales, you're usually only dealing with one other person. Usually, you're selling somebody something that they may or may not need to ask their significant other for buy-in or approval. While this can be challenging, in the world of B2B sales, it's often more complex and dynamic. With many clients, there could be three, four, or upwards of ten people in a large enterprise involved in a deal.

Even if it's not a service, there could be multiple departments involved and, therefore, multiple people with different objectives and different viewpoints. When they have different objectives and goals, that leads to wildly different objections that you need to be prepared to handle. They're not all going to have the same objection.

Work Your Prospecting Muscle

The best way to master addressing objections is to prepare for the different types of objections by practicing your responses.

One way I practiced was with flashcards. I would recall objections from my own customers, identify the five most common closing objections, and put them on cards. Then I would practice how I could best reply to those objections. When those objections made an appearance with prospects, I was not caught off guard because I already had some ideas for how to reply.

In prospecting, you're typically going to experience the following objections:

- I don't have time right now.
- I don't have a budget.
- I'm not the decision-maker.
- I'm already working with another vendor.
- You're not on my supplier list.
- It's just a bad time.

If you're starting out in sales, your ability to handle objections should improve greatly after the first four to six months on the job. The reason for this is because you're focused on improving this skill or working this muscle. When you begin a new job, you often have more resources in front of you, along with force-fed training and practice. When you pair that with an early desire to fill your calendar with appointments, you'll get fairly strong at objection handling purely through forced repetitions.

Unfortunately, some salespeople stop prospecting once

they have a few clients. Later on, they run into challenges with being able to handle objections that they faced because they haven't worked their prospecting muscle.

Imagine an amateur golfer who only golfs six months out of the year. Every year when they resume the game, their skills are rusty because they haven't been practicing consistently enough. A professional golfer is going to practice all year long and continue to develop the necessary skills. It is the same in sales.

Most salespeople go through high points and low points of prospecting. They'll do a lot of prospecting and then don't do any at all for a period of time. While it's understandable and necessary to work on existing deals, it can also be the biggest detriment to long-term success. Pausing new business development goes against the entire philosophy of this book —you need to constantly be feeding your funnel, feeding your pipeline, and building it.

Objection Immunity

Nobody likes to be rejected in the first place. If you can't get over rejection in sales, you're never going to succeed. Our job as salespeople is to be rejected roughly 90% of the time. The only way you're going to really get over objections is to put yourself in situations where you're rejected more often. You need to develop immunity to it, so it doesn't bother you anymore.

One young woman I was coaching was really struggling to hit her forecasted quota and activity numbers, but I didn't understand why until I started making sales calls with her. As we made calls together, I noticed that she was really struggling. Anytime she faced a prospecting objection, she would completely freeze. What I realized was that she had been avoiding making sales calls because she never learned how to deal with objections and took them as personal rejections. As you could imagine, this lowered her confidence substantially and, in turn, her results.

Her fear of rejection paralyzed her actions. Her fear of rejection lowered her sales call output, which didn't allow her to gain immunity to the feeling of rejection.

I encouraged her to face her fears by being more prepared and making more calls to experience more rejection. Once she started facing enough objections, she didn't fear them nearly as much and was able to stay calm. She realized that she needed to focus on addressing the objections, rather than shutting down and giving up. Once she figured that out, prospecting became much easier for her. Over time, by just running into more objections, she became more confident, quickly started growing her sales numbers, and hit her quota.

Don't Take It Personally

When someone tells you no, it can feel very personal. However, to the prospect, it is just a conditioned response. They don't know you and you're bothering them, so they object to talking to you. Even though it may seem rude when someone tells you no, it's not because they're trying to hurt your feelings.

When you are calling somebody, whether it's a cold call or a warm call, most of the time, the reason they're objecting to meeting with you or giving you any more time is that you're interrupting them. They are used to most salespeople completely folding. When they say, "No, I'm not interested," or "No, I don't have time," or "No, I'm already working with another vendor," that is just the status quo. They're conditioned to do that because most people will just feel rejected and give up.

Later on in the sales process, a prospect might object because they don't want to make the wrong decision and look like a fool in front of their boss and potentially lose their job.

Their objection isn't about you. When they're objecting, they may have a fear that is highly emotional and highly personal, which is why they don't want to go all-in on your product and tell their boss that this is the one they want to buy. It's possible that you've not uncovered the root cause of the problem, and likely haven't asked enough questions up to that point.

At the end of the day, if you've done your homework and know that your solution will solve their problem, don't take it personally when they object. Instead, focus on asking a great question to understand the concern, address it, and move on while helping them recognize that they are making the right decision by working with you.

Avoid Emotional Reactions

The biggest thing we can do for ourselves as salespeople is take a moment and realize that not responding emotionally is the best thing we can do. An emotional response can be saying, "Okay, I'll call you another time," because we've been rejected. They told us no, and we feel like we bothered that person. That's a hundred percent emotion talking to us. It's not rational decision making.

Our brains operate very, very slowly. While they process information quickly, they don't necessarily process it at the same speed as we speak. So when someone tells us no, naturally, our emotions kick in, our heart starts racing, our blood pressure rises, we feel insulted, it feels personal, and we're very quick to say, "Oh, okay, I'll just call you another time."

Other times, we may become defensive and argumentative. With objection handling, you should never argue with a prospect. Telling someone that they're wrong will never help you win in any situation. Most people know that, but they do it anyway. They find themselves arguing and refuting what someone tells them.

A better approach is to pause for a minute, take a breath, give your brain a chance to catch up, and then respond by agreeing with the person. So if they say, "Hey, I'm in the middle of something right now," you can agree by replying with, "I certainly understand. Everybody I work with is in the middle of something when I first call them." That throws off the pattern. Often, the best way to get through to prospects that are objecting is to interrupt the patterns they are used to.

Reducing Objections

There are things you can do to prevent objections from happening as often. Have clearer and more specific messaging when you call somebody. Prepare in advance so that you can have a tailored message. Be very specific about who you are, what you do, the problem you see, and the outcomes you deliver. Naturally, you're going to get better results. Most salespeople you are competing against are selling with a generalist mentality, treating all of their customers the same. This is a major reason why their results suffer.

You can't completely prevent objections. They will happen no matter what you do. Because as humans, we like to object to things that are different from what we know. However, if you're prepared, it allows you to prevent that objection from coming up altogether. Because you connected some dots for the person already, they can make more logical decisions. You help them work through that process in their brain ahead of time, so the objection doesn't even happen.

Mirror with Questions

Mirroring is an FBI negotiation tactic that Chris Voss references often in his book and training seminars. Mirror what someone says by repeating their language back at them. If they say, "Thanks for your call, but I'm okay right now," you can respond, "You're okay right now?" Responding this way may not feel right, but it is actually one of the best things you can say. This question prompts the prospect to elaborate so that you can learn more about their situation.

When someone says, "I'm already working with another vendor," you may not know what that means. You might assume they don't need you and just hang up. However, what if you asked, "Another vendor?" They might say, "I've got a vendor that provides a solution that does X, Y, and Z." Maybe that has nothing to do with the solution you provide. In fact, your solution may be a great add-on to the solution they already have. However, if you don't ask the question, you'll never know that.

Just because someone objects, don't assume you know what they mean. Often, our prospects don't really know how to articulate what they're trying to say. As an example, the common objection, "I'm already working with another vendor," could be completely made up. By mirroring the prospect, the prospect will often elaborate on their position, and you may find out they're not even working with a vendor that competes with you. They were just brushing you off because they didn't want to talk to you. If you always assume that you understand, you're going to find yourself in more situations where you don't give yourself the opportunity to address the objection. The prospect might actually be interested in meeting with you. It's just that you had to ask the next question to clarify their response and your understanding.

Get Good in Silence

In addition to asking follow-up questions, make sure you take time to pause. When talking to our customers, they're often not trained in how to object properly. So if you just simply let them object and continue to just listen, they will elaborate. This will help you have a better understanding of what the actual issue is. Then you can respond more appropriately and help them work through that.

Seek to Understand

Showing empathy for your prospects removes the pressure of the situation. Let them know that you understand where they're at. They're more likely to open up to you to explain their position.

If someone seems to be unable to commit to another meeting and says, "I don't want to invite other people to the meeting right now because I think you and I should just spend time talking further," you would say, "I totally understand that. It seems like you're under a tremendous amount of pressure, and I certainly don't want you to feel like you're not prepared to invite other people to our meeting. What additional questions can I answer for you that you might have right now that will help you feel more comfortable?"

Don't Give Up

Just because something is difficult, doesn't mean it isn't worth doing. In sales, you are always going to work with people who are difficult. In my career, the one thing I've noticed is that prospects who were the most difficult to acquire often became my favorite and best customers. I just had to try long enough and use different methods with them. At first, we often don't fully understand. Seek to understand, build rapport, and establish trust over time.

I once had an executive at a Fortune 500 company I had been calling on that I had identified through prospecting with lower-level decision-makers. This man held the keys to the castle. I tried over and over again to get a meeting with him.

My epiphany came when I realized that he wasn't going to remember me because other salespeople were calling him, and I was just another blip on the radar. I made the decision that if I was going to reach out to him, it was only when I had something of value to offer him. Up to that point, what I was focusing on just hadn't been a priority for him. So I never called, emailed, or texted him unless I had thought through my message and why I thought it would be important to him.

My messages were always very specific to him, his organization, and problems that existed in the industry and potentially for the company he worked for. I kept trying and eventually talked to some other people in the organization about what was important to him. Through leveraging other people for information and reading their annual report, I was able to put together a different message, which I found was tied to his top priority.

One day, I finally got him to respond through a text message in the late afternoon. I was able to set up a meeting with him that eventually led to a deal that helped me achieve over half my annual sales quota that year. It took me roughly nine months to make that connection. I realize most people would have given up earlier on. I took the responsibility to make sure that I wasn't annoying him as I always tried to lead with value.

Sometimes you're going to need to handle multiple objections with the same individual over the course of a nine-month sales cycle, especially to reach an executive decision-maker above the power band. However, over that time, they're not only going to see and appreciate your persistence, but they're also going to understand that you're not giving up. It may not happen right away, but that person may end up being your perfect customer in your career or for a lengthy period of time because you've worked through a lot of these issues and barriers that they've held up. Once those walls come down, people can become extremely loyal to you.

17

PERSISTENT PATIENCE

I n my second year of B2B sales, I was coming off a successful first year where I'd broken numerous mid-market accounts, yet I had just fallen short of hitting my goal and achieving our company's version of President's Club. I remember how frustrated I was because those that achieved the goal were awarded an amazing getaway trip to Mexico and a large bonus. I felt discouraged, but at the same time, I felt a fire inside of me.

At the time, I wanted to get back to a six-figure income after seeing a lot of success in the mortgage sales industry. B2C financial services sales are very different from selling to mid to large enterprises, so I had my work cut out for me. What B2C sales did teach me was to pick up the phone regardless of whether I liked it or not. Having an unparalleled work ethic is a requirement in sales and really any career you want to be successful in. In my first year, the quantity approach was working as more dials meant more interactions with prospects. Eventually, I started running out of steam as I started having prospects hang up on me or tell me to stop bugging them.

Imposter Syndrome had started to set in, and I was

beginning to wonder if I was cut out for strategic sales. I had many thoughts running through my head at that time, including whether I should go back to a more transactional selling industry. I'm not the giving up type of guy, so I committed to keep going and see what I could make of my second year. When I started the year, I was given a new territory. I began by building a list of the top potential customers, using a very similar approach as outlined in this book. I did a ton of research on each company I was prepared to call on. I carefully studied their annual reports, read their websites, and followed their social media accounts for information.

At the time, the top target account I wanted to break into was a Fortune 500 company that we'd not done business with in over eight years. I was excited about the opportunity to crack the code and break into the account. We knew the company was spending millions on services like ours and was ripe with opportunity. I knew if I could find a way in, I'd hit my goal for the year.

For the first three months, I called every prospect on my list using phone, email, and voicemail sales cadence spread out over the course of each week and month. I started gaining traction when I got my first opportunity to help a woman whom I'd met a few times. That was until someone in the procurement department stopped the engagement as they said our old contract from ten years prior was inactive, and they weren't looking to add new vendors to their supplier list. I was beyond frustrated as I knew that the procurement organization had given us trouble in the past and was the main reason prior sales reps weren't able to make any traction with the account over the years. I started to wonder if the time I was spending prospecting the account was worth it.

While I discussed the purpose of the sales campaign in a broader nature in Chapter 3, it is equally important to note that you have overall account sales campaigns that are broader in nature while also leveraging a campaign with each individual person inside the target account. As such, a campaign isn't a one-time event; it's ongoing. Not all prospects are ready to buy now, nor do you want to spend an exorbitant amount of time with a prospect if you determine they don't fit your ideal customer criteria.

Over the last decade, I've had many prospects that I have qualified out as potential future customers in the near term. There were red flags I could see that would prevent me from helping the customer, or they weren't ready or able to take action at that point due to a variety of circumstances I uncovered through my discovery. However, how you set the stage with the prospect in your initial interactions may greatly define the potential for them to become a future customer if you follow up with them over time by consistently adding value and differentiating yourself through the intelligent consultative selling strategies outlined in this book. Businesses are dynamic, and the tides can change quickly in small to large organizations. This can quickly turn a prospect that isn't ready to take action into a prospect that is your perfect customer. "I'm good" today can turn to "I need help" tomorrow.

The Bigger Picture

For most salespeople, their frustration with their lack of success builds too quickly, especially early on in their sales career. Understandably so. Sales is a numbers game, and you are measured on the points you put up on the scoreboard. If you don't score, you don't get paid and neither does the company. I've often wondered how differently salespeople would operate if they were measured and compensated differently. Would they take more time with prospects and build deeper, more meaningful relationships leading to easier and bigger sales? It's a question that may always go unanswered. It's difficult to come up with the perfect solution that drives the right level of high activity and urgency while still teaching sales reps to look at the bigger picture and exude some patience. As the saying goes, "Rome wasn't built in a day."

While prospecting and meeting with unqualified prospects can be a huge time suck, it's important to look at the long game in sales. Essentially, what is the long-term opportunity with a potential customer or your target market? It is up to you to determine if the effort and time are worth it. This decision is one that many salespeople struggle with because the consequences can be catastrophic on one's end-of-year sales numbers eating up our most precious resource: time.

Spending too much time attempting to create opportunities when roadblocks are too steep to overcome is a poor business strategy. On the other hand, give up too soon, and you may miss the opportunity to change your year or even your life. The best way to make these decisions is to leverage the information you gather through research and conversations with people inside and outside your target customers. Often, we give up too soon due to a lack of information to make well-educated business decisions.

Well-Informed Decisions

Before we determine if a prospect is or isn't worth our time, it's best to evaluate what we know about the person and company we are selling to. Here are some great questions to help you make well-informed decisions:

- Is the company spending or contracting?
- What percentage of their operational and capital expenses were spent on products/services in my industry?

- What are the company's business cycles and fiscal year end dates?
- Who are the incumbent competitors?
- How long have my competitors been doing business with my target customer?
- How long is their contract?
- Can the contract be broken?
- Who owns the contract?
- Who holds the relationship with my competitor?
- Who are the final decision-makers?
- Why would the prospect want out of their current contract?
- Do I know the different buyer landscapes in the account and the personas within them?
- Is the business issue or need great enough that something catastrophic will happen to their business if they don't invest in outside help?

Find Balance

At first, it is likely that you don't have all the answers to these questions. That's okay. Nobody does when they first start prospecting a potential client. What's more important is to take the time to uncover this information. For example, if a company recently signed a new multi-year contract with a competitor of ours and our product is generally sold to one specific department or persona within an organization, it is highly unlikely they will cancel the contract within the next year. Does this mean you should turn your back and prospect elsewhere? The answer may surprise you as it's a double-edged sword. The answer is actually yes *and* no.

In business, our performance is generally measured in shorter term increments, be it quarterly or annually. For this reason, it does make sense to prospect elsewhere as we must close sales with buyers that are ready and able to take action now. It's unavoidable. In fact, you should prospect many accounts and many people consistently, at all times. It's the name of the game in sales and the simplest way to build a consistent overflowing pipeline of business. It's all about filling the funnel!

Whoever gets in front of the most prospects with the ability to say yes usually wins. However, a smart seller would leverage the best of both worlds. Work the long game while simultaneously looking for buyers more ready to make decisions now. Some prospects don't need as much warming up. Some prospects are easier to build trust with more quickly. Sometimes, we connect with the right person with the perfect level of authority, influence, and power to make decisions. Sometimes we get lucky and our product or service is the absolute perfect fit at the perfect time, and we strike gold. Smart sellers focus on the now while consistently building for the future to land the whale client. They continue to collect new information and set appointments to understand what's going well and possibly isn't with the incumbent vendor. They build deep trusting relationships, so that they understand the prospect's business inside and out.

By being direct and upfront with prospects and sharing with them that you are standing on their sidelines cheering them on and there for them if they need you, they will respect you. It begs the question, when we lose to another salesperson or company, how long were they prospecting the account before they landed the sale? Often, the answer is a very long time. In order to go from good to great in sales, you have to play both the short and long game. It's the persistent, consistent, and patient effort that allows the world's best sellers to dominate their industry.

Whether you are selling to small businesses or large enterprises, success doesn't always happen overnight. As Jim Rohn stated, "Success is neither magical nor mysterious. Success is the natural consequence of consistently applying the basic fundamentals." While you may have heard that you should only spend time with prospects who are ready to buy now, it should be fairly obvious by now that I don't subscribe to that philosophy. If I did, I wouldn't have accomplished much of anything in my career.

Businesses go through many cycles, and people come and go in organizations. The larger the company, the more often this happens. You may find yourself with a slew of prospects willing to buy from you, yet you are unable to engage in business due to contractual issues. You may also find yourself calling on prospects that are deeply engaged with a competitor, and while you know you may provide a superior product or service, you are left outside looking in because they are unwilling to change or give you a shot. Until they are. You may have been sold the idea that money is made in closing deals. While it is true that we don't get paid until we ink the deal, I can assure you that most sales are made through consistent, patient, and value-packed follow-up over time.

Remember Relationships

What about the company whose procurement team shut me out? I ended up blowing that account up. I sold them multiple service offerings and hit my yearly goal. Guess who ended up inviting me to the dinner table? Procurement. Why did this happen? Well, after I was shut down by them, I realized I had made a critical mistake. I didn't have a relationship with the procurement and supplier management organization. I had no idea what they wanted to accomplish or how their goals were measured. I only felt that they were shutting me out because they were being difficult and controlling. "Typical procurement people," I told myself at the time. When I uncovered this mistake, I spent a few months meeting with them and getting to know their priorities, metrics, and challenges. I uncovered that the reason they weren't letting us engage in business was that they were rationalizing their vendor list. We weren't being considered because they thought we lacked the specific capabilities they needed to address their business goals.

Once I was able to help them see that their information was aged, and we did not only meet their minimum required capabilities but also provided more, something changed. They began asking me for input on certain areas of their business where they were struggling. Eventually, I had the opportunity to again ask for the business, and they gave me a window to deliver for them. Of course, I doubled down and made sure we delivered top-notch service. That opportunity led to nearly one million dollars in profit within a twelve-month period. The lesson here is simple. I spent over six months attempting to gain an opportunity, and it took another six months to realize that value completely. Had I turned my back on the company only searching for greener pastures, I would have never hit my sales goal for the year.

If you're reading this book, I can certainly guarantee you've had similar challenges or you will at some point. We all do! Trust the process. Businesses are run by humans. Humans pay to solve problems or help themselves. If they aren't ready yet, you either didn't do a good enough job asking questions to lead them to the epiphany that they need your help or, more than likely, they just weren't ready yet.

Rejection is part of sales. It's not personal. It's not because they don't like you. It's because they don't share the same perspective or have the same priorities as you. The moment that I started treating prospects and customers like human beings instead of a means to an end, everything changed for me. Being real works. People are smarter and savvier than you think.

Wouldn't you appreciate someone's grit, determination, and unwillingness to give up on attempting to help you if they consistently added value? You'd probably hand them your money after some time. I know I would.

Sometimes, all we need is time. If you have decided to make sales your career versus a job, you've got many years ahead of you. Act like it. Work your tail off to hit your near-term goals, but take your time and stay consistent. Your job is not to run people off the road. Leaving a path of destruction behind you does nothing but hurt your brand and your reputation. On the other hand, taking the approach I just outlined will get you a consistently overflowing pipeline where you can decide which opportunities you want to invest more time into and the ones you don't. The powerful feeling of turning away business is a strong sign that you're well on your way to reaching all of your goals.

Go get the next one, but don't forget about the last one.

Prospering Through Prospecting Action Step

You now know everything you need to know to begin using The Intelligence Factor! Go to your *Ready. Aim. Fire Workbook* and complete the exercises and questions for Part IV. Within the workbook, complete the calling with confidence self-assessment, reflect on how you address objections, and complete exercises that will help reset expectations and acquire the mindset needed to stay persistent in your pursuit of success.

To access your complimentary *Ready. Aim. Fire Workbook,* go to www.TheIntelligenceFactor.com/freeworkbook

AFTERWORD

Congratulations on making it this far! Give yourself a big pat on the back and smile wide. Finishing this book from beginning to end is a daunting task. That in itself puts you in a club of high performers already. You have now completed what I believe to be the most comprehensive book ever written on modern B2B sales prospecting. You have shown that you possess the level of commitment necessary to be widely successful in your career in sales. If you've been following along in the *Ready.Aim.Fire Workbook*, then you are already well on your way to reaching the upper echelon of sales professionals. If you didn't grab a copy of the workbook, you can get your complimentary copy at www. TheIntelligenceFactor.com/freeworkbook

It's important to remember that simply reading a book will not yield the results you desire. Earning a high six-figure income and more is possible if you put in the required work. Sales is one of the most challenging yet rewarding career paths you can choose. Whether you're just getting started in sales or you've got years under your belt, remember that nothing works unless you do. All successful careers are built upon years of hard work, effort, and learning from the failures you experience while continuing to push forward. As a sales professional, you will undoubtedly experience many ups and downs in your career. I have experienced many failures and hardships myself. Nearly all of my failures I have caused myself or were made worse due to my own mistakes.

While I've been very successful, there is one thing I know for fact: everyone can achieve similar success if they are willing to make the necessary sacrifices and put in the work. This includes you. Whether you're brilliant or an average Joe like me, you now have the tools necessary to achieve everything you desire in your sales career.

Now that you're armed with modern-day sales prospecting techniques that have created millions of dollars in revenue, it's time to start taking immediate and consistent action. Start dreaming of how differently you're going to show up with your prospects and customers. What will that look like? How will the trajectory of your career change?

Throughout your learning process, you will get rejected by prospects. We all do. No matter what you do, always remember that rejection is not personal. You must learn to ignore the emotions that come with being rejected. From this point on, you now understand that the top sales professionals you admire focus most of their attention on continuing to build their pipeline, always keeping it full of new opportunities. There is nothing more important in your quest for success.

As you continue on in your journey, you may look for more resources to help you along the way.

For those interested in accelerating their results even faster, you may be interested in my leading B2B sales training course, *Intelligent Sales Secrets Academy* (I.S.S.A.). This course is packed with every sales strategy and techniques I use today to close millions in sales year after year and consistently reach the top 1% of my industry. You can check out the course at www.intelligentsalessecretsacademy.com

Whatever you believe is or isn't possible in your life is what will become your reality. It all starts with you. Dreaming about the goals we want to achieve is a critical part of the journey. But just having goals is not enough. As my childhood idol, Michael Jordan, once said, "You have to expect things of yourself before you can do them."

What are your expectations for yourself? Are your actions mirroring your expectations? If they are, then you are on your way to achieving your goals. If you're on the other side of the fence, it's not too late. But it is time to level up, right now.

Starting right now, make the commitment to yourself to take full ownership of your sales career. No more limping through your day and going through the motions. You have the tools necessary to grow a massive pipeline that yields consistent game changing sales results. No matter how skilled you are naturally, you must put in the work. At this moment, start expecting greatness from yourself, refusing mediocrity, and fully committing to the actions necessary to help you reach and exceed your goals. You owe it to yourself and your loved ones to be great. You have it in you. Be different. Be great.

ACKNOWLEDGMENTS

If you would have told me twenty years ago that one day I'd author my first book before I turned forty years old, I would have never believed you. I still can't believe that all my failures and successes in life have led me to this point. As a boy who grew up dreaming of shooting fadeaway jumpers like M.J., I had to find a way to feed my competitive spirit. Sales became my north star—my vehicle, my passion, and my way of providing for my family and future generations after I am gone. If I had never found a career in sales, I don't know where I'd be.

I have been given multiple gifts in life that have allowed me to accomplish what I have thus far. Most of all, an unshakable mindset of doing whatever it takes to achieve the goals I've set out for myself. And while it feels good to speak of our work ethic, the ability to grind out through the hard times, and embrace the suck, the truth is that none of us achieve anything of substantial value alone. I have been afforded the opportunity to work with great people along the way.

While there have been many books written on what it means to be a great leader, I have found that leadership has shown up in a variety of different ways from different people throughout my life.

To my mother and father, thank you for providing me with a life of love, encouragement, and leadership. No son could ask for better role models in his life. I love you.

To my wonderful mentors and leaders over the last fifteen years, thank you for everything. The impact you've had on me professionally and personally is phenomenal. I value our relationships more than you'll ever know.

To my clients, thank you for trusting in me to do the right thing for your best interest. I've always prided myself on integrity and partnership. I hope you feel that you've been a recipient of that mentality and effort. Thank you for your partnership.

To my readers and students, thank you for trusting in me to read my first book! I am grateful for you and hope that my words and strategies are massively impactful on your career and life.

To my children, you are my purpose in life. Everything I do is for you, and I hope that my work makes you proud. Daddy loves you.

Most of all, I'm forever grateful to my beautiful wife Edith. You are the most devoted mother and wife I could ask for. I am thankful every day for having you in my life and you as the mother to our children. Thank you for putting up with many very late nights, early mornings, and often, an overly tired husband. Nothing I do in business is possible without your partnership and support. I love you.

ABOUT THE AUTHOR

 Erik Fisher is the CEO and founder of Intelligent Sales Secrets Academy. He has been featured in numerous media outlets including Thrive Global, Disrupt, Yahoo Finance, ABC, NBC, and FOX. Erik is a graduate of Illinois State University. He cut his teeth in professional sales in the mortgage industry, working for a large US bank as his first job out of college. While he was awarded numerous times for his leading sales performance, amidst the 2008 financial crisis, ultimately Erik decided that a path in B2B sales was where his future lay.

A serial sales professional and trainer, Erik continues to enjoy working for a leading IT services firm for the last twelve years, where he's won numerous awards as a top 1% producer. Erik's research-based approach to selling is anchored by the belief that prospects and customers open their minds to sales professionals with whom they have long-term relationships. His approach is anchored by an intelligence-based method whereby the seller focuses on specific, targeted, value-packed messaging and problem-solving techniques tailored to each unique company and individual.

Over the last decade, Erik has been afforded the

opportunity to amass over $40,000,000 in sales through a long-term, intelligence-based approach with the nucleus of strategy centered around delivering world-class customer experiences. Erik believes that all sales professionals can not only earn and leave a lasting financial legacy for their families but, equally importantly, deliver massive value to customers that solve modern-day business problems.

Through his methods, Erik has created a best selling B2B sales training program offered to individual sales professionals teaching the exact modern-day strategies he uses to open the doors to the most sought after clients in the world. His training can be found at

www.intelligentsalessecretsacademy.com

You can also connect with Erik on Instagram, Facebook, YouTube, Twitter, and LinkedIn, where he shares free weekly sales content.

Erik is a husband and father of two who advocates for Down Syndrome and other special needs communities. He is an avid golfer and fitness enthusiast who enjoys spending time with family and friends.

NOTES

Preface

1. Frost, Aja. "75 Key Sales Statistics That'll Help You Sell Smarter in 2020." *HubSpot Blog*, blog.hubspot.com/sales/sales-statistics

1. Your #1 Enemy: Fear

1. Cline, Damon. "Local Author Advocates Becoming 'Rejection Proof'." *The Augusta Chronicle*, The Augusta Chronicle, 29 Nov. 2018, www.augustachronicle.com/news/20181128/local-author-advocates-becoming-rejection-proof.

7. Friend or Foe? Knowing Your Competition

1. Villafañe, Camila. "10 Steve Jobs Marketing Lessons and His Famous Marketing Quotes." *Postcron*, 15 Feb. 2018, postcron.com/en/blog/10-amazing-marketing-lessons-steve-jobs-taught-us/.

10. Don't. Get. Stuck.

1. Larsen, Gabe. *The Definitive Guide to Sales Cadence: How to Double Your Contact Rates in Less Than 30 Days.* InsideSales.com, 2018.

12. Messaging

1. "ProvenModels - AIDA sales funnel - Elias St. Elmo Lewis." *ProvenModels*, www.provenmodels.com/547/aida-sales-funnel/elias-st.-elmo-lewis/.

14. Live Phone Messaging Framework

1. Bergland, Christopher. "The Neuroscience of Empathy." *Psychology Today*, Sussex Publishers, 10 Oct. 2013, www.psychologytoday.com/us/blog/the-athletes-way/201310/the-neuroscience-empathy.

2. "The Neuroscience of Giving." *Psychology Today*, Sussex Publishers, 24 Apr. 2014, www.psychologytoday.com/us/blog/vitality/201404/the-neuroscience-giving.
3. Voss, Chris, and Tahl Raz. *Never Split the Difference: Negotiating as If Your Life Depends on It*. Random House Business, 2017.
4. Nichols, Ralph G., and Leonard A. Stevens. "Listening to People." *Harvard Business Review*, 27 Nov. 2019, hbr.org/1957/09/listening-to-people.

15. Calling with Confidence

1. "A Decade of Digital Dependency." *Ofcom*, 8 May 2019, www.ofcom.org.uk/about-ofcom/latest/features-and-news/decade-of-digital-dependency.
2. Klingberg, Torkel. *The Overflowing Brain: Information Overload and the Limits of Working Memory*. Oxford University Press, 2009.

Made in USA - North Chelmsford, MA
1226910_9781949696127
01.20.2021 0852